WHAT IS YOUR PSI-Q?

WHAT IS YOUR PSI-Q?

OPENING UP TO YOUR PSYCHIC SELF

PETEY STEVENS

H J Kramer Inc
Tiburon, California

Published by H J Kramer Inc
P.O. Box 1082
Tiburon, CA 94920

Library of Congress Cataloging-in-Publication Data

Stevens, Petey.
    What is your psi-Q?

Bibliography: p.
1. Psychical research.   I. Title.
BF1040.S74   1989   133   88-91463
ISBN 0-915811-16-2

Editors: Gregory Armstrong and Nancy Carleton
Cover Art and Design: Francesca Angelesco
Typesetting: Classic Typography
Book Production: Schuettge & Carleton

Manufactured in the United States of America
10 9 8 7 6 5 4 3 2 1

When asked by his first grade teacher, "What does your mother do for a living?" Solomon replied, "She is a psychic." His teacher then asked him, "What does that mean?" Solomon answered, "That means that she is magic and she sees the magic in people!"

What Is Your Psi-Q? *is dedicated to all who believe in their own magic.*

To Our Readers

The books we publish are our contribution to an emerging world based on cooperation rather than on competition, on affirmation of the human spirit rather than on self-doubt, and on the certainty that all humanity is connected. Our goal is to touch as many lives as possible with a message of hope for a better world.

Hal and Linda Kramer, Publishers

Gratitudes and Acknowledgments

A heavenly host of relatives, friends, co-workers, contributors, editors, and publishers, through love, support, and guidance bring you this book.

Thank you Mom, Carol Renton Baldwin, whose faith and love for me has taken many shapes and forms as I've grown into Petey.

Thank you my four children, Heather (17), Solomon (13), Sarah (11), and Cassieoppia (8), for being my babies, my family, my teachers, my healers, and my special link to what is truly important to me . . . love.

Thank you Binta Daffeh for healing my environment and maintaining a semblance of order in our home. Your kind heart endears you to our family.

Thank you Mr. M for your faith in me, in my work, and in Heartsong. Without your support, I could not have written this book.

Thank you Lisa Wolfe-Held and Mary Menztel for being workmates and soul sisters who share the dream of Heartsong Center. Thank you Judith O'Connor; your loyal friendship and ability to live the Heartsong method continues to inspire me.

Thank you Heartsong students. Your number ranges somewhere between 18,000 and 21,000. You have come from all walks of life, all ages, and all races, creeds, and colors. You have had readings, healings, and regressions; you have taken classes and workshops. Some of you have studied in depth for several years. Thank you for sharing your psychic openings with me.

Thank you contributors for sharing your personal stories. For some of you, this was a ground-breaking experience. Because of you, our readers will understand the realities of the psychic opening process.

Three hip, hip, hoorays to Greg Armstrong, Hal Kramer, and Linda Kramer. The private time you each spent editing and cheerfully supporting me guided me through parts of my brain I didn't know existed! You literally taught me how to present my work while encouraging my own truth to come forward. All the love and support you each give to me is a writer's dream come true.

Contents

Exercises, Figures, and Charts

EXERCISES, FIGURES, AND CHARTS

Preface

Have you ever wondered if you possessed psychic powers? Does it ever seem to you that you are able to read other people's minds? Do you frequently experience synchronicity, meeting the very person you have been thinking about or finding exactly what you wanted in the most inexplicable place? Have you ever felt you were able to influence future events?

If you answered yes to any of these questions, chances are that you are psychic. Almost everyone is to some extent. Would you like to find out just how psychic you really are? Would you also like to find out what *kind* of psychic you are? Because there are many different kinds. Simply grab a pencil and paper and take the Psi-Q Test in Chapter 1 of this book. (Psi, for those of you unfamiliar with the term, simply means "having to do with psychic events and powers.") Take the test with yourself, or a special friend. Invite others over and have a Psi-Q party. Share and compare your answers as you open up your psychic self.

And most of all, would you like to develop your psychic abilities to their fullest extent? Learn how to help yourself and your friends by accessing the legendary powers of the psychic domain. Would you like to make a contribution to the spiritual growth of humanity? This may sound like a tall order, but at Heartsong, the school I run, I have taught over 20,000 men and women to do just that. In this book, I have distilled the essence of my successful teaching methods.

1

What Is Your Psi-Q? will introduce you to a variety of paranormal abilities that are ultimately available to all human beings as a part of their innate human potential. You will discover that seemingly normal thoughts, emotions, or sensations are often psychic occurrences. When consciously controlled, they become psychic abilities.

Just a word of warning. Developing your psychic abilities is not a parlor game. Psychic abilities are not just fun, even though they are probably the most enthralling of all human endeavors. Developing your psychic powers and learning to use them responsibly is a very serious undertaking, one which involves not only training in psychic abilities but also acquiring a whole new approach to life. True psychic powers involve far more than mere tricks. Psychic powers emerge and develop as a result of the highest and most deeply moral and spiritual way of life. True psychics are not entertainers. They are models of complete human beings.

It is in this spirit that this book is written. This book is intended for people who are willing to devote considerable time and energy to the undertaking. No greater rewards can be granted to anyone. But commitment is the price you must pay for the acquisition of psychic power—commitment to yourself and to your own personal growth.

The purpose of this book is not only to help you identify and develop your psychic abilities through the Psi-Q Test and the exercises throughout but also to help you develop your full human potential. I offer this book to share the work that has made my life so clear and happy. Join me in this pioneering work, and begin to develop your full potential. Expand the boundaries of your own reality. Yesterday's magic is today's experiment, and will become tomorrow's science.

May the wings of your spirit join the heart of your body!

Petey Stevens
Albany, California
1988

Introduction

Psychic: Defined and Demystified

psychic (si'kik) adj. [< Gr. psychicos, of the soul, spiritual < psyche, the soul: see Psyche] 1. of or having to do with the psyche, or mind. 2. beyond natural or known physical processes. 3. apparently sensitive to forces beyond the physical world. Also psy'chical. n. 1. a person who is supposedly sensitive to forces beyond the physical world. 2. a spiritualistic medium. psy'.chi.cal.ly. adv.

Webster's New World Dictionary, 2d ed.

We Are All Psychic!

Psychic abilities are not a special gift bestowed on a chosen few. Psychic abilities belong to the universal human potential. You can develop them just as athletes and dancers develop physical excellence while they condition their bodies, or as intellectuals develop mental prowess while they condition their minds.

Within all of us lies dormant the power to use our own soul's psychic intuitional nature. Psychically developed people have emerged in almost every culture in every century. In certain eras, psychics have been treated with respect and honor for their abilities; in others, they have been treated with fear and hatred. Through the centuries, awesome magical or paranormal powers have been attributed to psychics.

Some of the oldest stories of psychic powers come from Plato,

3

who told of the famed and lost continent called Atlantis. He suggested that the Atlanteans perished at their own hands from
the misuse of their psychic powers. The ancient Egyptians
also acknowledged psychic powers, consulting Winged Pharaoh
priests and priestesses who were capable of visiting the world
of dreams and of the dead, the Netherworld. Their psychic
powers were often exploited by manipulative leaders who sought
subconscious control over people. The ancient Greeks and
Romans recounted stories of magnificent gods and goddesses
with superhuman powers. Quite probably, these gods were in
fact highly developed psychics, who may have been as bewildered
about their abilities as their fellow countryfolk. The Greeks and
Romans also sought advice and direction from mystical psychics
called oracles or the Fates. They felt that their destiny was determined by the gods and goddesses and passed on to them through
the oracles.

Jesus Christ was also believed to be psychic. He himself said
that he ruled over a kingdom that was "not of this world." His
kingdom was that of his immortal soul. To autonomously reign
in his own soul's kingdom gave Jesus access to his psychic/
spiritual potential. He gained extraordinary spiritual maturity,
exhibiting deep, compassionate healing abilities and an unwaver-
ing altruistic and forgiving nature. Loved and followed by many,
he was eventually killed by those who misunderstood his powers
and statements of autonomy.

The father of medicine and originator of the Hippocratic oath,
Hippocrates, was an open and practicing psychic. He avowed:
"A physician without the knowledge of astrology has no right
to call himself a physician." He believed, as most psychics do:
As the macrocosm, so the microcosm. By understanding the
larger whole, we can understand our smaller individual selves.
Healing with the help of the stars and other natural elements
was practiced in other parts of our globe by tribal shamans.
African tribes practiced ancestor worship, which eventually
evolved into voodoo healing rituals in Haiti. In South and Central

America, tribal Indian shamans could heal anything from weak kidneys to schizophrenia with tropical herbs and plants taken during ritualistic prayers to the spirits involved. Like the Greeks and Romans before them, whose gods and goddesses were associated with counterparts in the physical world, North American Indians prayed to the great sky and ocean spirits, attributing to them the powers of these natural elements. They also used magical chants to elicit power, protection, and assistance from their ancestors' spirits with the aid of power animals.

Lunatics, madmen, and mystics who were locked away in dungeons, cages, and closets during the Dark Ages in Europe were often in reality misunderstood psychics. Witches were burned at the stake in Europe and later hanged or drowned in Salem, Massachusetts, because people feared their psychic powers.

When Abraham Lincoln was president, he held séances in the White House seeking political direction. Once he had a precognitive dream depicting his own assassination. Both Mozart and General Patton believed they had lived before and attributed their special genius to training in a previous life.

Both Freud and Jung wrote about psychic occurrences. Sanitoriums, mental hospitals, clinics, and psychiatric couches are full of wide-open psychics who do not understand their sensitivities and are not in control of them.

Today, scientific experiments from all over the world have tested, measured, and proved the electromagnetic qualities of human and plant auras. Kirlian photography, performed with relatively simple alterations and adjustments to a regular polaroid camera, can produce pictures of the human aura. Tests in the United States and Russia have measured the effects of psychokinesis, psychic healing, and meditative states of consciousness. Biofeedback machines have measured alpha, beta, and theta brain waves, enabling patients to identify these different states, calm down nervous tensions, and reduce possible heart attacks.

In the face of this positive evidence, even modern medical science has begun to reconsider its skepticism. The same question resurfaces again and again: What enables one person to heal, while another with a similar disease dies? Even medical doctors are now looking for the connections between the body, mind, and spirit for answers about the self-healing process.

We have now entered what must be regarded as the most psychic age in recent history. Shirley MacLaine's books, which relate her psychic opening experiences with transchannels and planetary power spots, have sold millions of copies. During Ronald Reagan's presidency, Nancy Reagan consulted an astrologer for guidance in making personal-safety decisions. The strange and unfamiliar is fast becoming commonplace in our society. Movies about ghosts and spirit possession, such as *Poltergeist* and *The Exorcist*, have entered our group mind. Yoda in the *Star Wars* movies teaches correct development of psychic powers. The television series "Star Trek: The Next Generation" depicts a female psychic as one of the captain's chief advisers. Her special psychic abilities are highly valued.

More people than ever are attending classes and lectures to develop their psychic powers. Something very special is happening as the New Age dawns. This is a time when many will reach their psychic potential and live in their own soul's enlightenment.

Coming Out as a Psychic

The purpose of this book is to help all who have a sincere desire to develop their latent psychic powers to the utmost. If you have relatives or co-workers who would be threatened or alienated by your coming out as a psychic, for your own protection I would advise you not to tell everyone at first. Reveal yourself as psychic only after you have attained a good understanding of what part psychic awareness plays in your life. While you are exploring this, feel out your friends and co-workers. You might ask them what they thought of the Reagans consulting an astrologer or of Shirley MacLaine's books. Then listen. You will know soon enough what they think of psychics. If they are interested in talking about it, they will be just as excited as you to have found a friend to talk to.

As you begin to develop your psychic abilities, seek out classes where you can meet new friends to share your interests. Classes in paranormal psychology are often given at local colleges. Recreation departments, churches, and singles' groups sometimes have classes on psychic openings, soul mates, psychic healing, channeling, astrology, and palmistry. Most large cities have one or two newspapers especially dedicated to New Age classes in yoga, meditation, astrology, palmistry, color therapy, past-life regression, and psychic development. Choosing a class may be difficult for you if you are totally new to the field. If you need guidance, call the editors of one of the New Age newspapers and ask about the classes that attract you. Find out how long the teachers have taught and how well they are established in the community. The editors will usually be able to guide you to the more reputable classes and teachers. New Age newspapers are often found in restaurants, coffeehouses, college campuses, supermarkets, YWCAs, and bookstores. Bookstores can provide a gold mine of information on classes and teachers as well as books on the subjects that most interest you. Specialized bookstores often carry a wide variety of metaphysical and self-help books. Many New Age bookstores periodically host lectures by authors of such books. Once you have nosed around, you will be amazed at how many people are already living in the light of the New Age. Welcome!

Chapter 1

What Is Your Psi-Q?

Psi-Q Test

Directions. Write the numbers one through twenty-seven on the left-hand side of a piece of paper. Mark each answer by using the following code.

Never 1
Seldom 2
Sometimes 3
Often 4
Always 5

Take all the time you need to answer each question thoughtfully. The test should take approximately half an hour to complete.

1. Are you self-governing and committed to your own perceptions without being overly influenced by other people's opinions and ideas about how you should live your life?
2. Are you considered thin-skinned, overly emotional, emotionally out of control, or too sensitive?
3. Do you sometimes seem to have an endless supply of energy? Do others call you nervous or hyperactive?
4. Do you sometimes feel as though you have already experienced certain present-moment events sometime in the past, even though you cannot recall when or how?

9

5. Can you move an object solely by the force of your mind?
6. Are you forgetful? Do people tend to regard you as spaced-out? Does it sometimes seem as if you are outside of your body, watching yourself as if you were seeing a movie?
7. Do you daydream about past and future events?
8. Do you love yourself and others with a positive, forgiving attitude without requirements or preconditions?
9. Do you share openly in the suffering, pain, enthusiasm, joy, and life experience of others as if it were your own?
10. Do you feel at peace with yourself and others? Do you have a sense of oneness with the Whole God Spirit?
11. Does it ever seem to you as if you could "smell trouble" or "smell death"?
12. Does your tone of voice affect others? Does it disturb, soothe, catalyze, or inspire them?
13. Do you talk to yourself?
14. Do you hear voices or music or speak to guardian angels, spirit guides, or invisible friends?
15. Do you know what others are thinking as if you were hearing their thoughts inside of your head?
16. Do you have dreams of events before they happen?
17. Can you foretell future events?
18. Do you have keen insights about people and life situations?
19. Do you remember living in another century or have images of life in another time?
20. Do you have a special rapport and understanding of animals, plants, and other species of life?
21. Can you visualize scenes and events that are physically far away from you?
22. Do you have extreme personality shifts or mood swings?
23. Do you believe that you and others can heal themselves?
24. Do you get answers to emotional, physical, or mental problems without deliberately and rationally thinking them through to the solutions?

25. When you touch an object, can you get information about its history or about its owner or creator? Does it seem as if your hands are picking up the information?
26. Are you able to find underground water or minerals?
27. Does your handwriting change from moment to moment?

Test Scores and Results

To get your score, add up the numbers you have written in response to the questions. Your score will tell you which of the four psychic categories you belong in. If your score was 54 or under, you are a closed psychic. If your score was between 55 and 80, you are a dawning psychic. If your score was between 81 and 107, you are an opening psychic. If your score was between 108 and 135, you are an open psychic.

CLOSED PSYCHICS (SCORE: 0–54)

You are probably not ready for this book. It is highly unlikely that at this stage of your life you would derive any benefit from it. Make a note of it for future reference and come back when you feel yourself becoming more receptive. Just bear in mind that regardless of your present state of mind, you do have the power to be psychic. It is only a matter of desire and openness.

DAWNING PSYCHICS (SCORE: 55–80)

Perhaps it is hardest of all to be a dawning psychic. You experience all the disruptive aspects of psychic ability without gaining very much in the way of positive benefits. You are a bit like a child still in the process of being born. The pain can be quite excruciating. But don't despair. Learn to reap the rewards that are certainly due you. Have faith and move on to the next level by completing all the exercises in this book.

Edith Bunker, the wife of Archie Bunker on the "All in the Family" television series, was a dawning psychic. She was very unsure of herself yet had a quiet and steady curiosity about life around her. Her uncertainty led her to believe the negative and derisive comments made by her closed psychic husband, Archie. She was keenly aware of Archie's hidden sensitivity. Even though he was rude and gruff with her, she felt a great sympathy for him and took on his problems and emotions as if they were her own.

Edith also took on Archie's opinions, and yet she internally fought against them. She was not aware of her inner beauty or her special charisma. She was an extremely self-conscious, shy person. Despite her shyness, Edith's compassion and humanitarian standards and ethics always won out. She believed in God as taught to her by organized religion, and she desperately wanted to be a good person. She scrutinized her actions, constantly checking and balancing her opinions against those of others. Edith Bunker was the salt of the Earth, but she was a great trial to herself.

OPENING PSYCHICS (SCORE: 81–107)

The best example of an opening psychic is Shirley MacLaine, who has recounted her experiences in *Out on a Limb, Dancing in the Light*, and *It's All in the Playing*. As an opening psychic, MacLaine constantly questioned herself and her reality. She had already developed her physical and mental potential and was ready to investigate and develop her psychic/spiritual potential. Synchronistically, she was meeting those attendant magical people and soul mates who always guide and assist as midwives the opening psychic's intense journey. She was beginning to understand with certainty who she was as a soul being.

All the events and people around her were helping to awaken her consciousness. She was fast becoming self-realized. She was intensely aware of every experience. She knew that each experience had a reason for happening. Although she was not always consciously aware of the reason, she had faith that each experience was correct and important. She was becoming the God/Goddess of her own universe, believing that she was a small part of the larger Whole God Spirit.

OPEN PSYCHICS (SCORE: 108–135)

To manifest as an open psychic is the crown of human creation. This exalted state is the ultimate quest of all human development. There are very few truly open psychics in our world. If you are one, it is very unlikely that you are reading this book. I include this description simply as a role model of the ideal state to which we can all aspire. If you haven't yet achieved this state, don't despair. It can only be achieved by the most dedicated and sincere practice. But simply working toward this state of being is as valuable and rewarding as ultimately achieving it. Enjoy the journey.

Mahatma Gandhi is one of the few examples of a completely open psychic in our time. He overcame his lower, domineering self and grew into one of the most benevolent, altruistic, and compassionate psychics who ever lived. He used his intuition in proevolutionary ways that always benefited the Whole God Spirit. After conquering his lower needs, his higher aspirations were raised even higher by the many long hours he spent meditating in and out of jail. He was punished severely for the nonviolent rebellion he inspired. With great compassion for those others would call enemies, Gandhi was good-natured, friendly, and cheerful. He always forgave his abusers because he realized they were unaware of the karma they brought upon themselves. He accepted himself as the one true God/Goddess governing his own reactions and interactions with others, and he always demanded the highest and most benevolent behavior of himself. At the same time, he was forgiving of himself when he showed human weakness. He never asked of others what he could not do himself. He had no egotism regarding his personal greatness. His goals were outside himself. He had completely given himself over to goals for the good of all, and he accepted a special wisdom and direction from an internal guidance that over the years he had learned to trust. This inner guidance never let him down. In his darkest personal hours, he displayed a never-ending supply

of enthusiasm fueled by his own self-inspiring joy. He lived by
the values he taught. He was what is known as a seed psychic
because others learned by his example. He planted within them
the seeds of personal consciousness or light.

DEVELOPING YOUR PSYCHIC POTENTIAL

Your Psi-Q score is not a fixed number. As you perform the
exercises in this book and open up psychically, your Psi-Q will
increase. You may want to take the Psi-Q Test again after you've
finished doing the exercises in the book. You'll be able to see
how far you've come in opening up to your psychic potential.

Chapter 2

Opening Up to Your Psychic Self

The descriptions of personal opening experiences included in this book were written by colleagues, Heartsong staff, and students. Through these descriptions, they share their process with the hope of alleviating some of your anxiety and fear as you open up. You may identify with some of their stories and not with others. The psychic opening process is a different experience for everyone. Notice how the writers of these stories learned to control themselves and their lives by utilizing their own souls' psychic abilities and awareness. You, too, can find your own unique path to psychic opening.

Coming Home
by Anne Loss Brooke

Opening psychically is the act of coming home. It is the process of coming most fully and deeply into yourself. Opening up and coming home. Home to self, home to God, home to the life that gives us both passion and rest.

Coming home. How often I have heard that phrase. It is a metaphor with many meanings. Yet every time I hear it, something inside of me stirs. Somewhere in my remembering, I have been home. The feeling of home is elusive, like a distant dream from my past, or a future familiar feeling knocking on my heart. At such moments, I feel an incredible longing and yearn for that place of home. Home is a place where I feel safe and content, a place where I am relaxed enough to be most fully who I am. Home is where I trust enough to accept challenges and take risks. It is where I know that I am loved from a place of non-judgment. Home is where I can open my heart and listen fully to others. To come home is to reclaim my power, to reclaim what is mine by birthright. Those things include my wisdom, my innate knowingness, and my ability to trust myself as a whole and complete individual.

How do I identify this place of home? For me it is a sensation of deepening, a place of trust. Whether I call it psychic, spiritual, or just plain meaningful, it is a place I know. It is also a place I forget. I forget I am home, and so I have to remind myself again and again that home is me. Home is the true me, my soul.

The path of coming home is not an easy one, nor is there any guarantee that I shall find it. I can get seduced away from the path by my intellect or by my cultural background, which emphasizes science and high technology. I can forget the path home by listening to a formal education that taught me to reason without the foundation of centered intuition. When I do remember home, I realize that I am already there if I can put aside my own disassociation from myself and others. Yet I forget this, and, like a wanderer, I must travel through the realms of my own subconscious darkness to know again that place of remembering. It takes courage to make the journey homeward. There are many bends and twists along the pathway. The path may be obscured, mystical, and ethereal, making it hard to see the way. Sometimes, coming home requires that I let go of my rational senses. Initially, this was difficult for me to do. I needed one of those boosts from life to be nudged out of thinking and learn just to be. That's how my journey home began. I had to fall out the doorway of my own beliefs about the world in order to accept the process of psychically opening up and coming home.

My opening journey literally began with a fall. I did not make a conscious choice to enter the realm of the intangible. I had been living off the land in Down East, Maine. A stoneware potter by trade, I had put together a small homestead with some adventurous friends on acreage north of Machias. Reality was governed by the need for food and shelter, especially given the harsh realities of the Maine winters. One autumn, in order to help with finances, I took a position as a cook on a fishing vessel off the coast of Cape Cod, Massachusetts.

New England Decembers are cold. I wore rubber gloves and big boots in oil skins to work in that weather. Fishing trips entailed long hours of both fun and hard work. It was dark when we docked alongside the swordfish boat. It was also low tide. I grabbed a bushel of lobsters and headed for the small metal ladder that ran the seventeen feet up to the top of the wharf. My balance was good from months at sea, and I was no more tired than usual after our four-day run. But I had been having strange dreams lately, and troubles at home were constantly on my mind.

Lobsters are cool when they first emerge from the sea. They are also heavy. As I jostled my load of lobsters up to my shoulder, their green-blue bodies were twisted around each other. Carefully, I inched my way up the ladder. I took two steps, hoisted the basket, and took two steps more. At the top of the ladder, I grunted the basket up and over the cap rail. Glad to be done, I put my gloved hands on the last top rung before hoisting myself up onto the wharf.

To this day, I don't understand what happened at that moment. For some strange and unconscious reason, I decided to let go. I didn't slip in the cold, moist air, or scramble for a hold on the metal rungs. I simply let go. And the instant I let go, I was no longer in my body. I was floating in the air with an incredible feeling of calm and curiosity. I watched my body fall with a complete sense of timelessness. I felt content, relaxed, and watchful. I mused that if the body I was watching survived I would reconnect; if it didn't, I wouldn't. I felt no fear or anxiety or attachment.

Sometime later—it could have been months or years, for I had no concept of time—I observed my body hit the water tank on the back of the swordfish boat. The totally limp physical form of my body landed partly on an old tire, partly on a reinforcing bar welded onto the water tank for use in securing lines. The body, my body, hit and bounced slightly from the impact. The instant I saw my body bounce, I reconnected with it. I was fully conscious, minimally bruised, and aware that my world would never be the same.

When I experience something, it is added somewhere in my brain cells to my understanding of life. I am a meaning-making creature, and I develop and grow by making patterns out of my experiences. When I have an experience that does not fit the pattern, my brain searches ever deeper into the collective computer for a way to categorize my new reality. When I watched my body fall, there was no file to be found in my brain. I had no conscious memory of ever experiencing anything similar to what I had just witnessed. Yet ever after that I knew there was another world—and perhaps many worlds—overlaid upon my reality. I had spent much of my life viewing the world from a small and narrow window, and it was a rude awakening to suddenly see life through a larger frame.

We humans are meaning makers, and we are also choice makers. At this point, I could have chosen to pretend I didn't know what I had just experienced—spending time outside of my body! I knew how denial worked. Like the formation of a pearl, I could coat my recent experience with layers of denial folded gently and securely around the irritating sands of this new awareness. I could create a smooth, hard sphere that hid my fear and questioning from the world and from myself. I could look for people who would tell me to forget it, or who would explain that I was dreaming. But I knew the full truth of my recent experience. It was this truth that could never be taken away. It was in honoring this truth that I began to set one foot before the other on my tentative and rambling search for the pathway home.

Some argue that understanding brings knowledge; others say that action and experience are the keys to enlightenment. I say they go hand in hand. Understanding for understanding's sake leads nowhere, and action without conscience produces mountains that must sometimes be moved. How then do I make meaning out of my experience and challenge the understandings I have brought into the world so that I am free to choose different actions?

Because of my otherworldly experience, I chose to explore psychic work. I needed a way to communicate my experience to the world. I needed a language. Clairvoyance was a tool to help me organize my experience of this other reality. I found value in learning psychic skills. In addition, I discovered that through trance work, through paying attention to that voice within, I was able to connect with my spirituality in a practical and conscious manner.

"Look at your belief systems. Look at the pictures. Notice what is current for you and what is old. Look at where you first learned to be this way. Good. Now blow up the image. Dynamite it. Take a breath and let it go. Breathe in your own energy. Let go of what is no longer yours." I found myself in Berkeley, California, sitting in trance at the beginning classes on clairvoyant reading and healing at Heartsong. This was a far cry from my tangible day-to-day world as a New England potter and fisherwoman. Yet here I was, learning to recognize and take responsibility for the world I had created.

With my curiosity as a guidepost, I began my journey home by opening up to my soul self. Opening is an individual process; there are many ways to open, and this opening can take many forms. On my path, I needed to connect with a group or teacher for support while I ventured into the unknown. Opening required that I take a stand for myself and ask for help; this was a time of both giving up control and taking charge of my beliefs and my life. Opening involved learning to listen to spirit in a form I could hear. So there I sat at Heartsong, going into trance day after day, opening up the energy centers in my body and learning to focus my attention and my breath, and to raise the vibrational levels of my body.

I learned to pay attention to my beliefs. For the first time, I had a sensation that I could create what happened in my life through the way I thought about things, and through the placement of my attention. If my thoughts were filled with fear and anxiety, events would happen that scared me. When I trusted and let my thoughts be expansive and creative, exciting opportunities surfaced. I learned to meditate and go into a trance state where I could listen to my soul for information. My visualization center opened up, and I started seeing auras and colors. When I did psychic readings for others, I would get images that had meaning for them. In addition to information, an important part of these readings was the interaction between myself and the readees. I learned to speak and interact in a manner that was healing for the readees and that gave them the experience of connecting from a heart level.

One of my deeper learnings was to view others from a place of nonjudgment. When I did this, I was able to teach and do psychic readings that were filled with love and compassion. The interactions between myself and people I read were open and nondefensive. Because psychic information is very direct and truthful, it was sometimes difficult for me to share what I was seeing with others. Yet I was committed to both truthfulness and compassion. What made these readings a healing and positive experience for both me and the readees was the focus on the positive intent behind a behavior pattern, however negative it appeared to be, and the learning that came from the pattern.

I am not saying that learning was all love and roses. It was real, and my teachers supported me in becoming real. To me, to be real is to be open, honest, and truthful with compassion. In learning these lessons, I was sometimes furious, sometimes despairing. There were times when I hated going to sit in yet another reading and having to examine my beliefs about life. I often did not like the feedback I received because I had to examine another area where I had been acting blindly. That was the bad news. The good news was that I really trusted the process of clairvoyant learning and the guidance I received. I trusted because the learning all came from my own images and my own intuition. No one was telling me what to say or believe when I opened up my intuitive eye. I would speak about what I saw. When I got stuck in a reading, literally tongue-tied and unable to either see anything or to say what I was seeing, I would be guided by one of the teachers to remove the belief that was in my way and to continue the reading. The teacher's role was to insure that the information for the person being read was clear and said in a way that was most useful for that person's learning. When the reading was over, the readee would go home and the teacher would sit with those of us who had read and help us examine the places where we had had difficulty. These were important sessions, sometimes tearful and sometimes humorous. I learned to laugh at my behaviors and beliefs. My commitment to this process and the guidance I received allowed me to grow and change.

In addition to readings, there were information nights. These times were for personal learning. I would sit in trance with a large group of advanced students. I would open up my third eye and watch the information that came to me when the teacher spoke about topics such as auras, being grounded, and playing the victim in relationships. We examined all kinds of issues: family patterns, taking responsibility for ourselves, being empowered, areas of conflict, the difference between loving someone and being in sympathy with them, how to move energy through the emotional centers, and more. I learned to recognize truth and to notice when I felt I was not getting the whole story from someone. I also learned to trust my perception and not to give up my ideas because someone did not agree with me. I learned to identify what it felt like to be off center, perhaps ignorant in some way, in my response to someone. I learned tools to help me continue to deepen and grow in my life. The exciting part of all this learning was that it fit for me with my journey home. I felt I was learning to open my intuition and consciously call on my soul self. I felt the same quality of perception I had experienced when I left my body during the fishing accident. I felt connected with God, with some being who was both myself and larger than myself. I was excited to learn that I could connect consciously to this energy force by using the tools of trance and clairvoyance.

Clairvoyance, or the ability to see clearly, sometimes gets bad press. This comes from misuse of techniques, from misunderstanding, and from fear. For me, clairvoyance was a tool for remembering, and definitely a tool for finding the path home. Clairvoyance was the tool that anybody who was open to learning could learn. I saw, through reading hundreds of people and through studying with people of diverse ages and backgrounds, that psychic abilities are innate in each of us. They come from our intuitive centers, and, like a muscle, develop further with use.

I have used the word clairvoyance for simplicity. You may understand it as vibration or prayer or meditation. What I am really talking about is psychic perception. If we think of perception as vibration, we can begin to recognize that this vibration can influence our way of seeing, as in clairvoyance. It can also influence our ability to perceive from a feeling level, which is known as clairsentience. Hearing things, such as other people's thoughts or sounds or music, is known as clairaudience. I am strongly clairvoyant and clairsentient. I have learned to develop my clairaudience through practice. All these tools are vibrations or channels of the same language of psychic perception. All can be developed.

To develop these tools, I had to examine my life. I had to be willing to experience myself fully, including both my joy and my sadness. I also needed to look at the ways I hurt in my life and the ways I was unconsciously hurting others. The tool of clairvoyance helped me deal with these hurts, and learn to avoid passing them on. I learned to treat myself and others differently, coming more often from a place of nonjudgment and compassion. This is the work of coming home. It is the effort that follows the intention, and the process that gives substance to change. It takes time—enough time to suspend old learnings and allow room for new possibilities.

One new element was that I could not go back to sleep. Opening up was like awakening. Once I had awakened, I could no longer shut my eyes to my life. It was like deciding to be honest. Once I made that decision, every little white lie became a bug in my consciousness. I started communicating in a more truthful manner. Surprise, surprise! When I communicated truthfully, people responded. They shared their stories and their lives. We made a loop of interaction that enriched all of us. I became intrigued with communication, with that ability of individuals to express themselves and to commune with themselves, with each other, and with nature. I saw, too, that communication takes many forms. Studying clairvoyance awakened my hunger to know more about perception and communication.

I began to branch out and complement my trance work with physically integrated learnings. I entered a four-year training in body-based therapy and did work with improvisational theater and dance. I joined a trapeze/dance group and saw how movement is a form of communication. I studied singing and explored how sound moves energy through the body. I began to look at my surroundings through the pattern of vibration and waves— waves that moved, waves that repeated, and waves that flowed in harmony or disharmony. I sought ways to play with these patterns and to shake them loose. I looked at patterns stored as memories in the tissue of the body. I had not known these existed until they came to the surface of my consciousness when released through deep tissue massage. The play and creativity of theater and dance allowed my spontaneity to emerge. By meditating before I go into a therapy session, I can become more sensitive to vibrations, and I find that I am more responsive to others. In leading workshops, I often help people channel into their hearts and find the place of self-knowledge.

In working with large groups, clairvoyance has a very practical application. As a facilitator, I know that sometimes the group process will freeze or become muddied. Sometimes I freeze right along with it. In order to facilitate efficiently, I must quickly clear out my frozen vibrations and listen for the next step. When I open up this way, I trust myself fully and have the experience of information coming from someplace larger than myself. The results are often surprising and delightful. Finally, clairvoyance is fun. People can quickly grasp the basics and begin using clairvoyance right away because it is a tool that leads people back to themselves. A group can learn to resonate to a common vibration and develop a wonderful sense of connection and attunement. As a tool for creation, people can learn to visualize what they want in their lives and begin to manifest it.

Taking charge of my life was one of the paradoxes of opening psychically. I began to see that I was not in control. There were other forces in nature that I could not move with my will. I had to pay attention and listen to these. Often I hoped that with just one more lesson, one more experience, one more piece of information, I would arrive. Then, I would be free. But the truth was that opening led further along the pathway, and I came to realize that life's meaning was being on the path and staying open to all of the experiences that came my way. Opening did not make life perfect, but it could provide the strength and creative intelligence to cope with the beauty of day-to-day living.

After teaching and studying, it was time for me to integrate what I had learned into my living in the world. I left Berkeley and moved to an area not so used to "energy work" and non-traditional forms of thinking. This was both a hard and a good experience for me. I started teaching classes at the local YMCA in movement and visualization and found that people loved it.

People who had previously only experienced a sense of God when at church listening to a minister began to talk about listening to their own God within. Through the movement and trance work, elderly women found a new tool they could use to help with the pain in their bodies. I saw that psychic tools were transferable to people who did not identify themselves as New Age. All that was needed for learning were people who were willing to be curious, to explore, and to have fun. The classes involved much humor and laughter, as people reconnected in a deeper way with themselves. In addition to refining my teaching skills, in my personal life I learned about intimacy in relationship. I discovered that true intimacy with another could only come when I first developed intimacy with myself. I also rediscovered my love of nature. The place I had moved to was near beautiful water and trees, and I felt renewed being out-of-doors so often. I learned the value of listening to nature and to trees and animals. I shared a language that comes from spirit with my environment. I knew through listening how I was interconnected with the Earth.

So many learnings, each one another step along my pathway home. In taking these steps into the world, my knowledge had once again expanded. This is what happened when I began to listen within and to respond to what I heard. When I opened psychically, I could no longer pretend I didn't know that other realities existed. When I truly listened, I began to hear other energies, or spirit, which would help me if I asked. Once I had the experience of listening to spirit, I knew I was forever marked with this knowledge. To leave it behind and pretend it did not exist would create misery in my life. I could not pretend that I didn't know about communicating with spirit and with people on both tangible and intangible levels. I could also no longer pretend that I didn't know what happened to people when they were reminded to come into their own hearts. Through my work, I had witnessed people reaching into themselves and then out to each other. Again, so many learnings. I was eager to apply all these learnings, and I wondered how they would fit into my life.

I went into a period of meditation. I wanted to know myself more fully and to see how I fit into this world. The sense I got was that my role with clairvoyance was to act as a bridge between metaphysical and practical realities. I was to work with people who had not already made a conscious connection with their subconscious. To do this, I needed more skills. I needed to be able to communicate more fully on the verbal level. I entered family therapy training and a graduate program that focused on group process and communication skills.

Through connections, phone calls, and keeping my vision clear, I was striving to give shape to my dream of interrelating the psychic and the practical. Little by little, the threads have pulled together and I have come full circle. The learnings I discovered about family therapy were actually a repetition of what I had already learned. The family therapy model I used looked at intergenerational legacies, patterns that have been passed on that we follow even though they are no longer appropriate. This is exactly what I had learned to do while sitting in a trance—to view the learnings in my life through the lens of their origin, to look at past lives and the lives of my family ancestors. Through family therapy, I learned to differentiate from my family. This means to stand alone and be separate. At Heartsong, I learned to be responsible for my belief systems and to begin choosing the ones that fit for me. Who is to say that these are not two sides of the same coin? Both taught me to be alone and to deal with that aloneness so that I could discover that being alone really means to be "all one" with myself and with spirit, friends, and loved ones.

The paradox of aloneness was that it was one of those places where "I was but I wasn't." For me, accepting my aloneness led to expanding my circle of contact with others. I went from private therapy practice to working with a team of trainers and to cofacilitating trainings in team spirit and performance. I bring to this work my learnings related to communication of body/

mind/spirit as I face new challenges. Once again, I feel my excitement and passion. Most importantly, each circle of movement has brought me further along the pathway home.

Chapter 3

Who Are You as a Psychic Being?

Essence Energy/Your Color Ray

Psychics perceive and experience all vibrations of energy. All things in this universe are made up of energy moving at different vibrations. All life forms, places, and things are composed of tiny sparks of energy, each distinguished from all others by the vibratory rate of its energy.

Human bodies, cars, houses, clothing, and diseases are all made up of slowly vibrating energy in the physical dimension. All energy that composes physical matter can be perceived by the physical senses. Nonphysical, psychic energy moves very quickly and is perceived by the soul's psychic sensors. All thoughts, feelings, and mental images are constantly perceived by the soul and are just as real from the soul's perspective as cars, money, and houses. The soul considers these images to be part of the real world. Open psychics constantly perceive and live in both physical and spiritual reality. It is part of human potential to manifest control in both realms, the physical universe and the soul's psychic universe.

Psychics decode, interpret, and translate the energy around them. Psychic *knowers* simply know energy, *clairvoyants* see energy, *clairaudients* hear energy, and *clairsentients* feel energy. Open psychics move with ease through their different realities because they can distinguish their own energy from everyone else's. They are aware of which thoughts, opinions, feelings,

ideas, judgments, and considerations are theirs and which belong
to others. This energy identification insures autonomy, free will,
and safety while opening up.

The following exercise will introduce you to your soul's
essence energy, allowing you to distinguish your own personal
energy from everyone else's. While you are doing the exercise,
be aware of the way you receive your psychic information. Do
you know it? See it? Hear it? Feel it? After the exercise is over,
match up the colors or attributes you experience with the Color
Chart that follows the exercise. Some people call their soul's
essence energy their color ray.

Essence Energy Exercise

1. Sit in a straight-backed chair with your hands and feet
   separated and your eyes closed.
2. Let go of all expectations about this exercise.
3. Begin to notice your breath. With every inhalation, imagine that you are inhaling your own soul's very personal
   and private essence energy through your mouth.
   Postulate that with every exhalation you are releasing
   and letting go of energy that does not belong to you. Inhale yourself, exhale all others. Inhale more of yourself
   and exhale more of others. Continue to inhale and exhale, filling your chest cavity and then emptying. Inhale
   and exhale, filling your lower torso and then emptying.
   Inhale and exhale, then breathe your own essence energy
   into your legs and feet while exhaling energy belonging
   to all others. Inhale more of yourself into your arms and
   exhale all others out of your arms and hands. Finally, inhale into your head your own soul's essence energy and
   exhale the essence energy of all others.
4. Did you *know* or *see* a color in your mind? If so, what
   was the color in your mind? Did you *hear* any words
   describing a color? Did you *feel* an emotion or state of
   consciousness? If so, what did you feel?

5. Maintain your own essence energy with your breath and postulate that from this moment on you will take in only your own soul's essence energy so that you can realize who you are and be yourself.

6. As you experience your essence energy, you will notice that you are not your physical body, you are not your car, your house, your thoughts, or your feelings. You are also not what others think or say about you. You are a soul, a divine and immortal being, a conscious energy unit in a vast pool of energy whose totality is the Whole God Spirit. You are the God/Goddess of your own personal universe, focused in time and distinguished from all other energy units by the vibration of your soul's pure essence energy.

7. End the exercise and open your eyes. If you saw a color, consult the following chart for its significance. This color is the color of your soul's essence energy.

COLOR CHART

Color	Shade	Characteristic Attributes
Gold	White Gold	Supreme Power
	Yellow Gold	Supreme Intelligence
	Pink Gold	Supreme Love
White	White	Purity
Violet	Lavender	Self-Esteem
	Violet	Enthusiasm
	Light Violet	High Aspirations
	Ultra Light	
	Violet	Spirituality

Purple	Dark Purple	Dogmatism
	Indigo	Religiousness
	Purple	Compassion
	Light Purple	Compassion
Blue	Dark Blue	Fanaticism, Seriousness
	Royal Blue	Devotion, Royalty
	Sky Blue	Clarity
	Silver Blue	Certainty
Green	Dark Green	Greed, Jealousy
	Forest Green	Growth
	Light Green	Calm, Quiet, Peacefulness
	Turquoise	Humor, Playfulness
Yellow	Mustard Yellow	Manipulation, Cowardice
	Dark Yellow	Intellectualization, Rationalization
	Yellow	Intelligence, Quick Wit
	Light Yellow	Wisdom, Light
Orange	Burnt Orange	Hysterical Emotions, Mischievousness
	Orange	Creativity
	Light Orange	Vitality, Healing
	Peach	Nurturing Love
Red	Wine Red	Negative Emotions, Hate, Anger
	Red	Passion, Stimulation
	Rose Pink	Hope, Optimism, Cheerfulness
	Pink	Love
Brown	Dark Brown	Negativity, Maliciousness
	Brown	Groundedness
	Light Brown	Earthiness
	Copper	Harmony With the Planet

Black	Black	Extreme Negativity,
		Frozen Energy
	Dark Gray	Depression, Apathy, Loss
	Gray	Confusion
	Silver	Power

Your Psychic Energy Body

Everyone has a psychic energy body as well as a physical energy body. The American psychic Edgar Cayce called this the astral body or second body. Russians have called it the bioplasmic body. The psychic energy body is made up of fixed and specific patterns of energy that regulate, organize, carry, and communicate your information and experiences. The mystics of India have identified the following components of the energy body: the aura and its boundaries; the energy centers, or chakras; and the psychic energy circuitry.

Psychics are open and receptive to all the energy in the energy body. Knowers know what is going on from basic energy intuition. Clairvoyants see the aura and the chakras, as well as symbolic images of experiences held in the aura and the chakras. Clairaudients hear the energy statements made about experiences in the energy body, and clairsentients feel the sensation of energy.

As you read the following information on your energy body, postulate, if you will, a complete second body made up only of psychic energy. This energy body contains colors and symbols and moves in an amoebic fashion. It has a skinlike boundary at its edge. It has circuit channels in the legs, arms, and back similar to the blood and nervous systems, and its chakras are attached into the back spinal channels and are similar to the physical body's glandular system. Healthy components of your energy body are as important to your well-being as healthy components are to your physical body.

AURA

Your aura is a magnetic field of energy that emanates from and surrounds your physical body. It carries your personal moods, dispositions, problems, and experiences. It is the same atmosphere that your soul radiates, changing from color to color and shifting its shape as it reflects how you hold, handle, and let go of life's daily experiences. Your aura is equipped to use only your energy. When you hold another's energy, opinion, consideration, or judgment in your aura, you will be blocked from developing your highest psychic potential because your consciousness will be focused away from your own growth and onto another's, which you cannot govern. You should be the only one in charge of your own aura. For your well-being, your aura should contain only your own energy.

AURIC BOUNDARIES

Your auric boundaries distinguish where you end and where the rest of the world begins. They are perceived by simply postulating that essence energy is somewhat denser at the edge of your aura. Then, like a spider's web, your boundaries will make you aware of energies around you. If you have ever felt "crowded in" by others, you are sensing the energy of their thoughts and feelings on the edge of your boundaries. You might experience a subtle sense of invasion, a sudden burst of intrusion, or an honorable, gentle acknowledgment. The sensations will vary with your life's experience. Boundaries are semipermeable, like the walls of a cell, to allow interactions and intimacies to penetrate within and radiate outward. Boundaries expand and contract in conjunction with your thoughts, feelings, and attitudes. When you feel threatened, your boundaries will pull in close to your body. When you feel safe, your aura and your boundaries will expand. Without boundaries, you would have no idea of who you are because your aura would have enmeshed with other people's auras. You would incorporate other people's thoughts, images, and feelings into your personal space, taking on their moods, experiencing their experiences, and acting out their opinions.

Aura and Boundary Exercise

1. Sit in a straight-backed chair with your hands and feet separated and your eyes closed.
2. Notice your breath. As you breathe, inhale your essence energy through your mouth and exhale all energies that aren't yours. Continue to take in more of yourself and let go of all energy that isn't yours. Fill up your legs, lower torso, middle torso, upper torso, arms, hands, and head with your essence energy and exhale all energies that are not yours. Fill up your entire body.
3. Continue to breathe in your essence energy and allow it to extend, one inch at a time, outside of your entire physical body. And continue to exhale all energies that are not of your essence. Breathe into another inch of your aura. Keep inhaling your energy essence inch by inch, until your aura has extended two feet outside of your body.
4. At your aura's edge, breathe about ten breaths or more in the same place until you have created a dense boundary. What does this boundary look like? What images does it elicit? Do you hear any sounds or words in your head? What does the boundary feel like? Postulate that when this exercise is done you will keep up your boundaries.
5. End the exercise.

What Kind of Psychic Are You?

The four main psychic types are the knower, the clairvoyant, the clairaudient, and the clairsentient. Each type receives information differently. Knowers simply know and have no reason or explanation for how they arrived at their knowingness. Some call the knower an intuitive. Clairvoyants see mental images in their heads. These images are sometimes lucid and clear like a photograph, and other times they are like cartoons. Clairaudients get their information in words and often in complete sentences or paragraphs. Clairsentients are feelers. They feel emotions and have actual bodily sensations that convey information.

The following exercise is to be done with a partner. Although eventually you will be able to sense, read, and translate an aura no matter how much is going on around you, I suggest that when you first try this preliminary exercise you do it in a quiet room by candlelight. Pick a time of day when you and your friend will not be disturbed. You will be distinguishing and separating out physical feelings and sensations from psychic feelings and sensations. Do not worry about translating or interpreting your experience. Just be very open and receptive to whatever impressions you pick up. Simply observe your psychic sensitivity.

Psychic Types Exercise

1. Sit in chairs opposite each other, with each of you breathing in your own private essence energies. Take turns completing the following procedures.

2. **Knowingness.** Postulate that you are a crystal radio and let yourself receive information about your partner's aura. Tell your partner anything that comes to you. Any color and any information you receive will be about your partner. During this exercise, you want only to know. If another ability, picture, words, or sensation comes up, simply ignore it and discover what you know to be true about your partner's aura. How big is it? Where does it end? To trust this process, simply accept it. When doubt comes up, breathe more of your essence energy into the crown of your head and breathe out the doubt.

3. **Clairvoyance.** With your eyes closed, picture your partner in the center of your head, just as that person is in front of you. Imagine an aura around your partner. Tell your partner what you see. What colors? What shapes? Where does the aura end? Does it have a boundary? Not

all people are clairvoyant, although this ability can be developed. If you do not see, you are blocked. The block can be released through your breath and your essence energy. Again, to trust this process is to accept it. Let it work for you. Breathe your essence energy into your head and exhale the darkness. Continue to breathe in your essence until you can see. You may only see a color or a symbolic image such as a lake with its boundary or a cloud with indistinct boundaries. These symbols would represent your partner's aura. Your clairvoyance will develop as you do the exercises throughout this book. Every image you see means something. After this exercise, you and your partner can investigate by communicating and discussing the images. Once I had an image of a certain tree come up in a reading, and I mentioned it to my client. Because I had no translation for the image, I didn't try to explain it. As I described the tree, my client started to cry. Her grandmother's house had had a big tree that she had climbed and sat in as a child. Her grandmother had just died and was very much on her mind. When you don't know the meaning of an image, simply describe it.

4. *Clairaudience.* With your eyes closed, listen to the thoughts and words in your head. What are they telling you about your partner? Say anything that comes to mind. Hearing voices isn't crazy! Many of us get our information through words and statements we hear in our heads. All this book asks you to do is listen consciously to the words. What are they saying to you? Some of the words are your thoughts; they are made up of your essence energy. Some of the words are your partner's and are made up of your partner's essence energy. Some are voices from your childhood, representing the energy of your mother, your father, or perhaps a childhood teacher. The voices will sound like the people whose

energy you are hearing. Understanding the voices is the
beginning. Trust that you are in a process of opening
and developing.

5. *Psychometric Clairsentience.* Focus all of your attention
   into the palms of your hands and rub them together to
   sensitize them to your awareness. Now stand up and feel
   your partner's aura with one hand. Start with your hand
   about three or four feet away and slowly bring the palm
   of your hand toward your partner. Do you feel anything?
   What do you feel when you run the palm of your hand
   about two inches away from and up the spine of your
   partner's back? Are any points more noticeable than
   others? Are you feeling any emotions such as fear, excitement, joy, or anxiety? When you are clairsentiently
   feeling another person, all the feelings you have at that
   moment are the other's emotions. Openly share what
   you felt with your partner.

6. Change places and repeat steps 1 through 5. You will discover
   very quickly how you receive information and what type
   of psychic perception is strongest in you—knowingness,
   clairvoyance, clairaudience, or clairsentience—by the
   speed with which you get your information. The quicker
   the information comes, the more open and developed
   your sensitivity is in that form of perception. Do not fret
   if you can hear but not know, feel but not see. Eventually,
   you will develop all of your psychic perceptions. Right
   now, you are experimenting to understand how you presently
   perceive energy, before you develop yourself further.

7. End the exercise.

Psychic Circuitry

Your psychic circuitry nourishes your energy body and serves
as a release valve, laundry chute, or plumbing system that lets
go of excess, foreign, or unneeded energies. The excretion system

is called your grounding cord and goes from the base of your spine into the center of the Earth's magnetic core. It is quite simply a beam or cord of energy connecting you with the planet Earth. It is your soul's conscious commitment to its own reality.

RUNNING ENERGY

All of our universe, including both our physical reality and our psychic/spiritual reality, is made up of energy. Our combined realities are like a large body of energy, or a vast ocean. We are each one cell, one fish. We walk on the planet Earth and in the psychic dimensions at the same time. Your physical body is nourished by eating food in your physical reality, while your psychic body is nourished by "running" energy in the psychic reality.

Your psychic circuitry includes energy channels in your psychic body. Geographically, the major channels correspond to your major bones. Channels go up your legs, up the spine of your back, through your head, and down your arms. You can deliberately "run your energy," choose its colors, and consciously control your moods, dispositions, actions, and mental states. You run energy through your body all the time. Why not take conscious control of it? No matter what color you bring into your body, continuously postulate that you are drawing from two pools of your own essence energy that are stored in the center of the Earth and in the center of the Cosmos.

You will feel definite sensations as you run your energy through your channels. When your energy comes through slowly, it will feel tingly, the same tingly sensation you get when your foot falls asleep and yet nothing is asleep and nothing hurts. A sudden rush of energy, called a kundalini experience, may feel very hot. Or you may experience a cooling or calming sensation in your legs and the spine of your back.

The following exercise will help you ground yourself and run your energy.

Running Energy Exercise I

1. Sit in a straight-backed chair with your hands and feet apart.
2. Breathe for a few minutes. Inhale and exhale, filling your aura up with your own essence energy. As your aura fills up, place your attention on the base of your spine. Allow a golden ball of your essence energy to form with a cord attached to it. Let the golden ball and the cord drop as a beam of energy down from the base of your spine through the many layers of soil, rocks, water tables, crystal caves, and molten lava into the center of the Earth's gravitational core. Allow the gravity of the Earth's magnetic force to draw your cord in. When the golden ball reaches the center of the Earth, it will fuse into the magnetic core. What body sensations or changes do you notice? Do you feel heavier or more solid? Do you feel a pull at the base of your spine into the core of the Earth?
3. Do you see your grounding cord? If so, what does it look like? Do you hear any information about your cord? Are you aware of disclaiming thoughts or feelings? Are you afraid? Ground anyway, even if you do not believe in the procedure.
4. Without removing your grounding cord, place your attention on the arches of your feet and bring a pink energy from the Earth into your feet openings. Allow this energy to travel up your leg channels and into your pelvic cradle. Hold the earth energy there for a moment.
5. Now place your attention on the crown of your head. Bring blue energy from the Cosmos into the back of the crown of your head. Pull the energy down the outer part of the spine of your back and into your pelvic cradle.
6. Combine, balance, and blend the earth and cosmic energies in your pelvic cradle. Allow the mixture of energies to run up the front part of the spine of your back and out the crown of your head. Allow the energy to flow

through you. Bring the earth energy into your feet and up your legs. Bring the cosmic energy into the crown of your head and down the back of your spine, and mix these energies in your pelvic cradle. Run your energy up the front of your spine and out the crown of your head. Allow yourself to flow with the current of the Universe. Notice how you get your energy information. Do you know it, see it, hear it, or feel it? What impressions and perceptions are you noticing? Maintain this energy flow for ten minutes.

7. Open your eyes when you are done. Now you are connected with your own source of soul essence, and you are grounded on the planet Earth. Anytime, anyplace, you can renew and refresh yourself by grounding and running your energy. But you have begun to accomplish more. You have actually begun to take control of your own psychic self. You have purposefully directed your soul's essence through your energy body. The control of this inner reality, your soul's reality, is not a simple venture, but you have already done it at least once.

8. End the exercise.

Practice grounding and running your energy every day. I do it for ten to twenty minutes three times a day: in the morning when I first rise, in the afternoon, and at night just before I go to sleep. Feed your soul as well as your body!

Shedding Skin, Shedding Light
by Vesela Shivick

Shortly after my twenty-ninth birthday, I was busy tending to Saturday chores and listening to the radio. My attention tuned in and out. I heard a woman on the radio speaking of her difficult adolescence and early adulthood. I turned the volume up and sat attentively, transfixed because the woman's experiences sounded so much like my own.

I now understand that a higher force was presenting me with my spiritual teacher. The woman on the radio was Petey Stevens. She talked about her opening, she interpreted the dreams and experiences of puzzled callers who phoned the radio station, and she urged listeners to visit Heartsong, the school and book-store she had founded.

Until I heard Petey describe her own path, I had stopped wondering if anyone else struggled with a temperament as sen-sitive as my own. Except for my mother, no one had admitted to a daily challenge with emotions. We resigned ourselves to temperaments out of sync with the times. When others would tell us that we were "too sensitive, too emotional, and too touchy," they told us nothing we hadn't already heard, and their judg-ments were to no avail because they did nothing to change our natural response to the world.

After listening to Petey on the radio, my husband, David, and I drove to Albany to visit Heartsong that same day. I wasn't ready for a class; I wanted to learn more about psychic phenomena on my own. Among the many books I found at Heartsong, I chose Petey's *Opening Up to Your Psychic Self.* David drove us home, while I began reading aloud to both of us.

By evening, I was ready to try some of the meditations pro-vided in the book. I carefully followed Petey's directions, recorded my impressions in the journal I was keeping, and went off to bed. David stayed up to work longer on his projects. Asleep in the bedroom, I suddenly awoke. I was lying on a futon close to the floor. Directly across from me, I saw a translucent green snake steadily approaching my bed. I panicked and tried to scream; I awoke as if from a dream. I ran to David, who was still work-ing in the living room, for protection and comfort. Safe in his arms, I resolved not to explore psychic phenomena any further.

Brought up in the Christian faith, I made the traditional as-sociations: snake, tempter, envoy of Satan, evil, danger. I thought that through my interest in psychic phenomena I had tasted the forbidden fruit, and I wanted no more of this frightening dimension. Although I set Petey's book aside the following day, my inward journey had begun. An invisible guide continued to lead me deeper within myself to learn the real import of the snake.

I sit here today writing this piece, overwhelmed by the many diverse experiences that marked my twenty-ninth year, the year of my Saturn Return, as astrologers call this period of transformation. I was "a dawning psychic," to whom timely teachers came in books, in friends, in visions, and in Petey and Heartsong. I have chosen to share the snake's lessons here so that you may know the soul's opening is real and so that you may trust this process, however frightening and disorienting it may first appear to be.

Not only had my higher self brought me to Petey that year, it had also wreaked havoc on my outer world. I was a high school English teacher who could not understand what had become of her short-lived career. Where I had once been able to foster an atmosphere of learning, fun, and harmony in the classroom, I no longer could. Something was wrong. Suddenly, I was not an effective, enthusiastic teacher. I lost my livelihood. David and I were creating a strong and loving marriage, but that was not enough for me. I didn't know how to fill the void inside myself. I felt useless and without purpose.

A series of synchronistic events led me to read Shakti Gawain's *Living in the Light* and Shirley MacLaine's accounts of her spiritual opening, and I began to study the tarot. I became convinced that I must quit my job, though I remained unclear about my life's direction. I only felt certain and impassioned about David and about my need to search within myself. I steadily read the metaphysical books that came my way, and I enrolled in Heartsong's psychic program. Satan be damned—that green snake could well have symbolized the victimization I felt in my world gone haywire.

I asked for understanding, and my psyche answered. In meditation class, we learned to run different colors through our energy body. One night at home, experimenting with different colors as we were told to do, I meditated and ran blue energy. In trance, I saw a cloud of blue that shaped itself into a serpent. I was afraid again, ready to jump back and pull myself out of trance. This time, however, my readings came to my aid. What I had read of archetypal images and inner visions taught me the importance of confronting my fear. I gazed steadily at the snake. It slowly changed, transforming itself into a bouquet of blue flowers. So much for that, I thought. Confront what you fear, and it becomes a gift. I believed the bouquet meant that I was growing and would soon flower in my psychic development.

Weeks later, another snake came to me in a dream. I was once again in my childhood bedroom; I was a teenager. My older sister was with me, and we talked as we used to do. She went into the bathroom to prepare for bed, while I remained, lying on my bed. Suddenly, I sensed danger and was afraid. A silver snake rose from the floor to the edge of my bed. In terror, I tried to retreat, but I was powerless to move. I closed my eyes and prepared myself for the pain of its attack. The snake touched my forehead with its tongue, and I was surprised—it didn't hurt. The snake's touch felt cool, smooth, and surprisingly soothing. I awoke.

I related this dream to Petey, who congratulated me; I had had a shamanistic experience. My inner vision, my third eye, was opening.

In the days that followed, still another snake came to me, this time in a meditative vision. I was sitting on my sofa reading *Seth Speaks* by Jane Roberts. Seth suggested a meditation in which you visualize yourself on a stage as the lights dim and you are left in darkness. The goal was to attend to the inner life experienced in this darkness. I did this and waited quietly, receptively. The drama commenced. A black serpent slithered its way from behind the sofa and around, again stopping in front of me. It raised its head to my level. It was huge—a black cobra with markings below its mouth, a white triangle with a red center. Its aspect was sinister. This time I was too scared to endure the confrontation; I opened my eyes and brought myself out of trance.

Frightened and confused, I didn't understand why snakes kept appearing before me. I thought the previous vision had eliminated my fear of the archetype. I sought counsel from teachers and friends at Heartsong. I learned that the snake was my ally, my power animal. It would continue to return until I assimilated its lessons. I needed to trust my psyche's process.

Again in meditation, the black cobra returned. I was sitting in a chair. It crept up from behind and slid into me, up from my tailbone and into my head. Its form was extended along and lodged in my spine.

Not long after this, I attended the Whole Life Expo in San Francisco. At a lecture on "The Modern Practical Value of Shamanism," I was guided in meditation by two of the speakers, James Swan and Lewis Mehl. I recorded my experience in my journal as follows.

I am looking out over the lake
toward the mountains and sky
when you come up from behind me.

Up . . . into my tailbone . . . through my spine,
your head joins with mine.

You and I are One.

We dive into the lake . . . cool . . . refreshing.

I enjoy using my arms to stroke . . . my legs to flutter.

You make this so easy . . . smooth . . . graceful.

Sinuous . . . energizing . . . propelling.

The night of the same day, I meditated while listening to a shamanic drum tape. I saw myself lying down in a desert. A huge rattler approached and swallowed me head first, as it glided on, until I emerged again from its tail.

With each of these experiences, my understanding of the snake's lessons grew; the snake taught me what I needed to know about myself at different times in my psychic development. The snake helped me to realize that at a deep level I feared life because I did not honor my deepest self. I wasn't meeting life's challenges and opportunities from my own center, but from beliefs and programs that I had assimilated from others: my family's desires and fears, my teachers' expectations, my peers' demands. It was time to honor my innermost self, my integrity, my soul. In doing so, I do not violate my love for others. With or without their acceptance, I live truly—with self-acceptance.

When the snake kissed my forehead, my third eye, it responded to my desire and promised the clarity of inner vision I sought. The snake went on to show me that my fears were opportunities for me to flower when I faced them honestly, from deep within my soul. I often feared others because I feared my own ego. Having seen others abuse power, I was afraid to assume my own. When it sought shelter in my body, in my spine, the serpent directed me to assume my power, to trust myself, and to love. Once I empowered myself, the snake showed me that I could live with freedom, grace, and creativity, confidently navigating the waters of my inner and outer life. Then the snake swallowed and released me, to remind me that life is a cycle of renewal— birth, death, rebirth. Once I stopped clinging to my outlived expectations, I would find myself adapting to life anew. As Joseph Campbell has explained so eloquently, the snake is a "terrible apparition of unmastered psychological energies."

My ally, the serpent, helped me to recognize and respond to my soul's needs. As I learned and integrated each lesson into my life, my reality became fulfilling and exciting again. David and I have altered our way of life because of our shared inward journeys. We no longer work frenetically to achieve a financial life-style that reassured others of our value more than it met our own desires. We live among the trees, as we had always wanted, and we make time for each other as well as for our personal interests. I earn money teaching bright-eyed preschoolers and then devote myself to my livelihood, writing and reading. We both remain committed to our psychic development, and we turn inward daily to discover how best to live wisely and lovingly on this wondrous planet of ours.

Recently, when we were out walking, we came across a dead baby rattler in the middle of the road. David respectfully buried it among the leaves and trees. I saw that the cycle was complete. We have shed our former skins to live in the sun with our new ones—with trust in nature's process.

Chakras

The chakras are energy centers that hold the deeper roots of your personality, expression, and experience. There are seven major and four minor chakras in your energy body. The chakra system allows you to categorize your psychic impressions and to organize your psychic abilities. It gives you a clear perspective of who you are as a psychic being. The chakras work together to help you as a psychic being not only to survive, but to feel, to be empowered, to communicate, to see, to know, and to have all of your psychic senses available for your use. Studying the chakra system is no different from studying a scientific, mathematical, or exercise system. The chakras work intrapersonally within the individual. They work interpersonally with other people's chakras, and transpersonally from soul to soul. Each chakra is like a cone of energy located at a specific place on your body. The pointed end is rooted into the spine of your back, where all your nervous system converges. Each chakra functions by sending, receiving, and organizing energy information as program disks do for a computer. Each chakra has physiological correlations, characteristic psychological and physical imbalances, as well as psychic abilities. You have seven major chakras to help run your body. They deal with survival, feelings, power, affinity, communication, vision, and knowingness. You have already used the minor chakras in your hands during the aura exercise in running your energy. Read over the definitions and functions of each chakra and take a moment to reflect on your own ideas and impressions of each one. Which information stands out for you? Are any of the details profoundly interesting? Are they confusing? Begin to know your own chakras as you read the following.

CHAKRA CHART
FIRST CHAKRA (SURVIVAL CENTER)

Location: Base of spine

Function: Sending, receiving, and organizing survival
information; grounding

Physiological Correlations: Ovaries, testes, placenta, bladder,
anus, colon

Physical Imbalances: Bladder problems, colon problems,
female reproductive problems, fluid retention, male
reproductive problems, sciatic problems, urethral
problems, yeast infections

Psychological Imbalances: Accident proneness, in survival
mode, dependent personality, identity crisis,
nervousness, weak ego structure

Psychic Abilities: Grounding

SECOND CHAKRA (FEELING CENTER)

Location: Center of abdomen

Function: Sending, receiving, and organizing emotions;
sensate feelings

Physiological Correlations: Insulin-producing glands,
appendix, intestines, kidneys, pancreas, spleen

Physical Imbalances: Anemia, allergies, diabetes, diarrhea,
duodenal ulcers, hypoglycemia, kidney problems,
leukemia, lower back problems, pancreatic
problems, premenstrual syndrome, spleen problems

Psychological Imbalances: Autism, chameleon personality, depression, dissociation from emotions, hysteria, inability to be sexually intimate
Psychic Abilities: Clairsentience

THIRD CHAKRA (POWER CENTER)

Location: Above navel
Function: Generator and distributor of personal energy; empowerment
Physiological Correlations: Adrenal glands, solar plexus neural center, autonomic control center, stomach, liver
Physical Imbalances: Absorption problems, adrenal problems, arthritis, anorexia nervosa, cancer, coordination problems, liver problems, multiple sclerosis, obesity, premature aging, stomach problems
Psychological Imbalances: Addictive personality, catatonic schizophrenia, compulsive behavior, excessive anger or fear, manic-depressive behavior, obsessive behavior, sleep problems
Psychic Abilities: Déjà vu, empowerment, telekinesis, psychokinesis, out-of-body experiences, time travel

FOURTH CHAKRA (HEART CENTER)

Location: Center of chest
Function: Equalizer, self-love
Physiological Correlations: Thymus gland, heart, vascular system, lungs, respiratory system, immune system
Physical Imbalances: Autoimmune problems, circulatory problems, heart problems, high blood pressure, lung cancer, lung problems, respiratory problems, thymus problems, upper back problems, vascular problems
Psychological Imbalances: At war with oneself, feelings of alienation, inability to bond with others, self-destructive tendencies, suicide
Psychic Abilities: Affinity, compassion, unconditional love

FIFTH CHAKRA (COMMUNICATION CENTER)

Location: Center of throat

Function: Sending, receiving, and organizing
communication

Physiological Correlations: Thyroid, parathyroid, lymphatic
system, brain stem, throat, ears, mouth, teeth

Physical Imbalances: Cancer, ear and hearing problems,
lymphatic problems, mouth problems, neck and
shoulder problems, parathyroid problems, speech
problems, dental problems, thyroid problems,
throat problems

Psychological Imbalances: Inability to express self in words,
logorrhea (nonstop verbal chatter), poor auditory
memory, stuttering

Psychic Abilities: Clairaudience, clairolfactory sensitivity,
tone healing, inner voice, telepathy

SIXTH CHAKRA (VISION CENTER, THIRD EYE)

Location: Center of forehead

Function: Sending, receiving, and organizing visions and
mental images

Physiological Correlations: Pineal gland, neomammalian
brain, greater left hemisphere, central nervous
system, eyes, sinus

Physical Imbalances: Brain tumors, cancer, central nervous
system problems, eye and vision problems, sinus
headaches, sinus problems

Psychological Imbalances: Extreme confusion, fixations,
inability to focus, intelligence deficiencies, living in
a fantasy world, paranoia, poor visual memory,
psychotic behavior, schizophrenia, severe
retardation

Psychic Abilities: Precognitive dreams, intuition, prediction,
clairvoyance, past-life recall, cross-species
communication, remote viewing

SEVENTH CHAKRA (CROWN CENTER, KNOWINGNESS)

Location: Crown of head

Function: Antennae

Physiological Correlations: Pituitary gland, old mammalian brain, greater right hemisphere

Physical Imbalances: Baldness, brain tumors, cancer, epilepsy, migraine headaches, Parkinson's disease, pituitary problems

Psychological Imbalances: Excessive gullibility, memory disorders, multiple personalities, nightmares, split personality

Psychic Abilities: Transmediumship, transchanneling, faith healing, intuition, knowingness

HAND CHAKRAS

Location: Palms of each hand

Function: Channeling creativity

Physiological Correlations: Hands, fingers, wrists

Physical Imbalances: Carpal tunnel syndrome, arthritis

Psychological Imbalances: Kleptomania

Psychic Abilities: Manifest creativity, psychometry, dowsing

FEET CHAKRAS

Location: Arch of each foot

Function: Connection to the Earth, channeling earth energy

Physiological Correlations: Feet, toes, ankles

Physical Imbalances: Athlete's foot

Psychological Imbalances: Inability to "stand on one's own"

Psychic Abilities: Connection to the Earth

Chakra Exercise

1. Sit in a comfortable chair with your hands and feet apart and close your eyes.

2. Breathe in your own essence energy for one or two minutes.

3. Ground yourself by breathing your essence energy into your pelvic cradle and allowing it to form a dense golden ball of energy and a large rope of energy around it. When your pelvic cradle is full, drop the golden ball with the rope or cord of energy attached to it down into the center of the Earth and run your energy using golden earth energy and silver cosmic energy. Place your attention on the arches of your feet and allow the golden earth energy to come into your arches, up your legs, and into your pelvic cradle. Now place your attention on the back of the crown of your head and pull in silver cosmic energy. Allow the cosmic energy to go down your spine and into your pelvic cradle. There the earth and cosmic energies blend and mix.

4. Now pull the combined earth and cosmic energies up the spine of your back, stopping at the first chakra, at the base of your spine. This is where all of your survival information is kept. Connect the cone-shaped chakra deeply into the spinal channels on your back and allow the mixture of earth and cosmic energies to flush through your first chakra, cleaning it out and energizing it. Take full responsibility for your survival and own your first chakra by saying out loud, "My survival chakra." What do you already know about your survival? What do you see, hear, or feel?

5. Place your attention on the center of your abdomen, where your second chakra is located. Connect this chakra into the spinal channels on your back and flush the energy from the channels on your back through your second chakra. Clean it out and energize it. Own it and take responsibility for your emotions and your second chakra by saying out loud, "My feeling chakra." What do you know, see, hear, or feel about your emotions and feelings?

6. Now move your attention up to within three fingers of your navel, to your third chakra. Connect this chakra into the channels on your back and flush out the chakra, cleaning and energizing it. Own it and take responsibility for your power and your third chakra by saying out loud, "My power chakra." What do you know, see, hear, or feel about your own empowerment?

7. Place your attention on the center of your heart and connect your heart chakra into the channels on your back. Flush out your heart chakra and energize it. Own your ability to love, and take responsibility for how you receive love, by saying out loud, "My heart chakra." What do you know, see, hear, or feel about your own self-acceptance?

8. Move your attention to your throat, where your fifth chakra is located. Connect your fifth chakra up to the back of your spine and flush out and energize your throat chakra. Own your throat chakra and take responsibility for your communication by saying, "My communication chakra." What do you know, see, hear, or feel about your own communication?

9. Place your attention on your forehead, the site of your sixth chakra. Connect this chakra to the channels in your back and flush out and energize your sixth chakra. Own your sixth chakra and take responsibility for your vision by saying, "My vision chakra." What do you know, see, hear, or feel about your psychic vision?

10. Finally, place your attention on the crown of your head and affirm the connection of your crown chakra into the channels in your back. Flush out and energize your crown chakra. Own your seventh chakra and take responsibility for your knowingness by saying, "My knowing chakra." What do you know, see, or feel about your knowingness?

11. Open your eyes and end the exercise.

Shaman's Mission
by Roderick Clayton

It took me most of my life to get past sneering at all things psychic as the domain of fortune-tellers and swindlers. I could have saved myself so much trouble—abuse of alcohol and drugs to dull "abnormal," untrained senses, worry that strange perceptions were some kind of mental illness, and the stress of transition between states of consciousness without understanding.

Like all small children, I lived in the world of magic, but when I was old enough to "know better," I continued to see, hear, and otherwise sense things that other people didn't. I soon learned to keep my perceptions to myself. Finding little joy in turning inward, I coped with stress by visiting a more restful place—outside myself. When I first heard of the process of "astral projection" described, I immediately recognized it as something I'd been doing since childhood.

In my life, psychic awareness has been wedded to religious experience. Over the years, I read many books about shamanism, usually anthropology books given to terms such as "witch doctor" and "superstition." Even these supercilious accounts managed to describe a comfortable and familiar aspect of my experience, which I now recognize as a shamanic state of consciousness, or astral travel/awareness.

I felt overwhelmingly drawn to the life and society of the people of the northern edge of the Pacific Rim—Kwakiutl, Inuit, and Siberian. However, shamanism appeared to flourish only where it was deeply rooted in its host culture. I concluded that I couldn't follow God in this way because I was born a Westerner.

Years later, I happily learned that I had been wrong. It's true that you can't make shamanism work independently of local culture. *You must change the culture* so that it welcomes its shamans. This entails getting people to want healing more than they want the false comfort of denial. The post–World War II generation has begun to move in this direction.

For a time, I volunteered at a crisis hotline. Lacking referral resources for anything short of suicide prevention, we quickly learned to improvise. Most callers were in emotional distress but unlikely to connect with a "real" therapist. I was overwhelmed by the responsibility of being the first, and maybe the only, available support person for very troubled people. Our callers' problems were not purely emotional; they were likely to be sick, destitute, homeless, or in trouble with the law.

Spirit guides showed me that I could best serve my clients not with my analytical mind (by interpreting their words), but psychically (by hearing the songs of their hearts). Obscure voices speaking ancient words told me that integrity means not just keeping secrets, but also coming from the heart, compassionately, whatever your opinion of your clients or their problems. I also learned that serving others is a privilege, not a duty.

One brilliant Sunday afternoon in my thirty-third summer, I sat admiring a daytime full moon. Suddenly, a hawk flew directly across the moon's face, wings spread voluptuously. He "spoke" to me (clairsentiently, not in words): "I've been assigned to you. Any questions?" I dismissed him as a pleasant vision until he returned, again and again, over the next several months, first in my sleep but later at other times as well. Again and again, he told me, "I'm not just a vision, I'm not the flashback you never had, I'm your *power animal*. I've been waiting for a long time to get your attention. I have things to tell you that God wants you to know, and I'm also here to remind you that God loves you and pays attention to you." My hawk has been a constant and welcome (if stern) companion ever since.

A few years later, I was fortunate enough to meet my first spiritual teacher, who taught me rituals for daily communication with my power animal, the four winds, and other totemic ("familiar") spirit guides. She also conducted a ritual "reintroducing" me to my spirit protectors as a prodigal son wishing to come home. Since then, I have performed these simple ceremonies twice a day, and I have been well rewarded for doing so.

For many years, I was a volunteer with an emergency medical

clinic that provided free care at public events, usually rock-and-roll shows. One of my duties was to "talk down" people who had taken too much of God Knows What (usually including LSD). I gradually learned to identify the drugs my patients had taken by looking at their auras. I was surprised to find that many of the doctors and nurses concurred with this approach!

When you talk someone down, you discover that your patients are generally "trapped inside." I would go inside, meet them "there," and lead or show them the way back. If you don't stay carefully grounded during this process, you can get into a lot of trouble doing this. For a long time, I didn't know how to stay grounded, and, more than once, my patients recovered, leaving me on their bad trips! Gradually, I learned to be a conductor, not a receptor, of psychic energy. This lets me ground for people who are temporarily unable to ground themselves, without making myself crazy in the process.

A gift emergency medical work confers, besides the possibility of saving lives, is the ability to enter a clear state instantly and on command, however tired or distraught. I originally thought this was just an adrenaline rush in a crisis, but I now know it to be a "threshold" shamanic state of consciousness in which energy is visible and pain is forgotten.

The true measure of your devotion to anything is not what you put into it, but what you take from it into the rest of your life. Serving and healing others gave me a place in a family, and the lifelong drive to be part of families whose members have walked long miles and faced hardship and danger together.

A few years ago, I followed millions of my contemporaries into detoxification from alcohol. Most will agree that this is an unparalleled occasion for spiritual awakening. The fragments of psychic/divine awareness and experience I had accumulated over the years assembled themselves into a pattern by which I could live my daily life. My psychic opening was finally "anchored."

Realizing I needed to find ways to connect astrally without using the drugs upon which I had come to depend (more for modulation than for establishing the connection), I recalled from earlier reading that drugs were nearly always secondary to ritual and meditation in attaining the shamanic state of consciousness. For example, the Jivaro and many Siberians usually used nothing stronger than tobacco.

My decision to "get well" was preceded by such pain and difficulty that I thought I wanted to die. On schedule, my hawk appeared and confronted me with the news, "I know what you want, but you do not have my permission. You have a mission as yet unfulfilled." Uncharacteristically kind, he did not push my face in the fact that I also had a son not yet grown.

Today I lead a pleasant if prosaic life. I earn my living as a programmer, as I have for the last twenty-five years. Most programmers and engineers know, and deny, that the toughest technical problems are not solved logically; the left brain just isn't big enough to store even a simple computer program all at once, and "intuition" usually saves the day.

Meanwhile, I'm happily learning to see chakras and auras in classes at the Heartsong Center, enjoying for the first time the comfort of sharing my experiences and beliefs with new friends traveling on old roads. Heartsong attracted me because it is not a cult or a refuge for those who can't or won't live in the world. It is a home for those who can and do live in the world as open psychics. Heartsong also embodies the idea of "new" and "made" families. Its members make themselves responsible for loving each other in ways that feed wellness and openness rather than fuel people's problems. I stay in close touch with my well-loved first teacher, mentioned earlier, whose perspective keeps me from developing too parochial an outlook.

I believe I am on the way to understanding and fulfilling the cryptic "mission" of which my power animal spoke. This mission involves developing and pursuing my psychic gifts, and I know in my heart that I am meant to do this while living *in the world*, not on some far-off mountaintop.

We must remember that, although psychic skills are learned,

psychic abilities are given by God. Not all of us are meant to
be great seers or powerful healers, but we all need each other.
Religion, to make sense, has to work in the real world for real
people. Those who are not seeking religion can still benefit from
our psychic/shamanic families and communities, much as many
non-Christians turn to established churches for counseling and
other forms of support. It is widely agreed, even by many prac-
titioners, that contemporary psychotherapy is almost at a dead
end. It costs too much and helps too few of those who do obtain
it. In many cases, it's a plaything for the idle rich. Meanwhile,
ordinary people are ever more in need of accessible, practical
ways to process everyday issues. Psychic healing is an obvious
and effective response.

The family/community/tribe model supports an evolving
culture that, I hope, will want true healing. We have a long way
to go. The field abounds with much that is trendy and super-
ficial. Nevertheless, this thin topsoil is already fertile ground for
psychic seeking and for the practice of shamanism. I'm grateful
to be spending my life helping to nourish that ground by being
part of newly developing families, communities, and tribes, drawing from and passing along their traditions.

Chapter 4

Psychic Communication and Interactions

Your psychic body comes complete with its own method of communication, a language of symbols, images, and sensations. You have already begun to experience this dimension of psychic energy in doing the previous exercises. A symbol represents something. The aura represents your reality, and its boundaries outline the part of your reality you control. The chakras represent the deeper roots of your behavior and personality. Your grounding cord represents your commitment to your life.

Psychic Pictures

Psychics speak in a symbolic language that employs what are known as psychic pictures. Psychic pictures are symbolic images representing an experience. Each picture has its own basic integrity, yet it is also colored by feelings and thoughts about the situation or experience it represents. When you were a small child, you took in reels and reels of pictures reflecting your perspective and memory of the daily situations you experienced. Pictures are the information chips of the energy body's computer program. They hold the original sources of our life attitudes.

Picture Seeing Exercise

1. Sit in a comfortable straight-backed chair with your hands and feet separated.
2. Breathe in your essence energy and allow your exhalations

59

to release any energy that is not yours. Breathe in and
clean out all body limbs, your complete torso, your head,
your chakras, and your aura out to your boundary's edge.

3. Allow your essence energy to form your grounding cord
by breathing more of your essence energy into your
pelvic cradle. When you have formed a golden ball with
a long cord attached to it, let the golden ball drop down
into the center of the Earth. You are now grounded.

4. Run your energy, using your own essence energy. Place
your attention on the arches of your feet and allow your
essence energy to flow up into your pelvic cradle. At the
same time, pull your essence energy into the back of
the crown of your head and down into your pelvic
cradle. Allow earth and cosmic energies to mix in your
pelvic cradle and go up the back of your spine and out
the crown of your head. Run your energy for five to ten
minutes before you go on.

5. Pull all of your conscious awareness into the exact
geographical center of your own head. Here, you will
find your soul consciousness. It will appear to you as a
bluish white light. Notice your mental image screen in
front of your position in the center of your head. This
screen is totally permeable and see-through and has a
grounding cord of its own.

6. Look at your visual screen and project an apple, a big,
lucious, bright red apple on the visual screen. Look at
the apple. See the apple in detail, as if it were really in
front of you. Then release the apple through a grounding cord attached to the screen.

7. Now visualize a flower, a bright red rose. Observe the
rose. Notice its color and its stem. Are there dew drops
on its leaves? Look closely at every detail, until you can
almost smell the rose. Then drain the image of the rose
down the screen's grounding cord.

8. Finally, visualize a glass of water. How full is it? Does it

have ice in it? Does it make you thirsty? See every
detail of the glass of water. Then drain the image down
the screen's grounding cord.
9. Drain the whole visual screen down its own grounding
cord, somewhat like a retractable movie screen.
10. End the exercise.

Some pictures are positive and recorded neatly in our memory
banks. Some are negative, holding or maintaining fear or trauma
you were unable to process at the time. Negative pictures are
traumatically bonded in your chakras. As if in shock, the electromagnetic current of energy is frozen until you are able to process these traumas. Traumatically bonded pictures seem to have
two distinct parts—the core picture, of the first time you ever
had the traumatic experience, and the reinforcing pictures, of
life experiences that reaffirmed your original, or core, picture.
You can process a picture by fantasizing, by thinking it through,
by talking it through verbally with a friend or a therapist, or by
entering a dream state. For instance, you may dream of a vic-
torious battle with a dragon or of winning a Nobel prize. A self-
affirming dream releases the negative charge from the picture
and files it in your memory banks.

The mechanics of processing a picture are simple. First, a picture is perceived by a chakra. Then, the energy of the picture
is transformed into a color representing its chief emotion. Each
chakra decodes energy differently. The seven chakras are to the
energy body as the five physical senses are to the physical body.

Seventh Chakra: You know the energy picture.
Sixth Chakra: You see the energy picture.
Fifth Chakra: You hear the energy picture.
Fourth Chakra: You are at one with the energy picture.
Third Chakra: You experience the power of the energy picture.
Second Chakra: You feel the energy picture.
First Chakra: You are validated by the energy picture.

The picture then travels through the channels on your back to the center of your head, where it is filed in your memory banks. All people, whether aware of their psychic abilities or not, read and decode pictures automatically and unconsciously by processing and organizing them in their energy bodies. Those who do this consciously are called psychics!

Processing Core Pictures Exercise

1. Sit in a comfortable straight-backed chair with your hands and feet separated.
2. Breathe in your essence energy and allow your exhalations to release any energy that is not yours. Breathe in and clean out all body limbs, your complete torso, your head, your chakras, and your aura out to your boundary's edge.
3. Allow your essence energy to form your grounding cord by breathing more of your essence energy into your pelvic cradle. When you have formed a golden ball with a long cord attached to it, let the golden ball drop down into the center of the Earth. You are now grounded.
4 Run your energy, using your own essence energy. Place your attention on the arches of your feet and allow your essence energy to flow up into your pelvic cradle. At the same time, pull your essence energy into the back of the crown of your head and down into your pelvic cradle. Allow earth and cosmic energies to mix in your pelvic cradle and go up the back of your spine and out the crown of your head. Run your energy for five to ten minutes before you go on.
5. Pull all of your conscious awareness into the exact geographical center of your own head. Here, you will find your soul consciousness. It will appear to you as a bluish white light. Notice your mental image screen in front of your position in the center of your head. This screen is totally permeable and see-through and has a grounding cord of its own.

6. On your visual screen, visualize a replica of your own energy body, with an aura, boundaries, and chakras hooked up into your back channels. Look at this grid of your energy body. Ask to "see" where on the grid a particular negative picture concerning your primary caretaker as a child is stored. A black dot will appear somewhere on your grid. Most likely, it will be near or in a chakra.

7. Visualize the black dot moving into and through the chakra located near it, proceeding into the spinal channels on your back. Run the dot up these channels into the center of your head to your visual screen. What do you see? Who is in the picture? Why was the picture originally stuck in or near that particular chakra? Pictures get stuck in or near the chakra that originally dealt with the experience they represent. A picture stuck in or near the first chakra deals with issues of survival. A picture stuck in or near the second chakra deals with emotions and sexuality. A picture stuck in or near the third chakra deals with issues of power. A picture stuck in or near the fourth chakra deals with issues of love. A picture stuck in or near the fifth chakra deals with issues of communication. A picture stuck in or near the sixth chakra deals with issues of image and vision. A picture stuck in or near the seventh chakra deals with issues of knowingness.

8. What do you know, see, hear, and feel about the picture of your primary caretaker? This is where you must take control of the negative charge or trauma of the picture. Psychically, simply drain the color, which represents the charge or traumatic emotions and sensations of the experience, down your screen's grounding cord. Let go of all of the color and emotional charge of the picture, leaving a black-and-white image in front of you. Then, release the words associated with the pic-

ture, letting them drain from the shades of gray in the image. Next, let go of the outline of the image, which represents the visual image itself, and, finally, release the frame around the image so that the screen is empty.

9. Now, visualize a large golden heart on your screen, to represent forgiveness of yourself for getting stuck and of your primary caretaker for triggering the stuckness. Then, watch the heart on your visual screen descend through your energy system and return to the exact place where the picture was originally stuck. You have now replaced the negative, dark picture with a positive, healing symbol.

10. Drain the images from your visual screen and allow the screen to retract down its own grounding cord.

11. End the exercise.

Cord Messages

Psychics also experience energy communication between their chakras. When two people are relating, they send cords of energy to each other's chakras. Some cords set up healthy, clear, and open communications and attachments with others; others set up unhealthy, restrictive, or manipulative bonds, with the intent of controlling others. The following chart shows some typical communication cords between chakras and what they mean. Many more cord combinations are possible than this chart shows, because people can send cords and communicate creatively from all chakras to all chakras. This chart simply shows basic cord communication.

CORD MESSAGES CHART

Chakra	Sends	Receives
7	I own you.	Own me.
7	Let's share knowingness.	O.K.

6	I see you.	See me; pay attention to me.
6	I see what you see.	See what I see.
6	I will see for you.	See for me.
5	Telepathic messages	Telepathic messages
5	Let me tell you something.	Tell me something.
5	Let me talk for you.	Talk for me.
5	Hear me.	I hear you.
5	I will say what you want to hear.	Tell me what I want to hear.
5	Let's communicate.	O.K.
4	I love you.	Love me.
4	I love you.	I love you.
3	I have control of your energy.	Tell me what to do.
3	Give me energy.	Take my energy.
2	Feel my emotions.	I feel your emotions.
2	I want you sexually.	Want me sexually.
1	I will save you.	Save me.
1	Keep me alive.	I will keep you alive.
1	Ground me.	I will ground you.

You may see cords visually. This is the most objective and clearest way. You may also hear the message they send in your head, or you may feel the attendant emotions or sensations when the cords plug into your chakra. If you get a sudden pain in your heart chakra, someone may be pulling a love cord out. If you feel a sensation of warmth, perhaps someone is plugging a love cord in. Physical sensations in the area of the chakras is often caused by the plugging or unplugging of a cord.

Communication Cords Exercise

1. Sit in a comfortable straight-backed chair with your hands and feet separated.
2. Breathe in your essence energy and allow your exhalations to release any energy that is not yours. Breathe in and clean out all body limbs, your complete torso, your head, your chakras, and your aura out to your boundary's edge.
3. Allow your essence energy to form your grounding cord by breathing more of your essence energy into your pelvic cradle. When you have formed a golden ball with a long cord attached to it, let the golden ball drop down into the center of the Earth. You are now grounded.
4. Run your energy, using your own essence energy. Place your attention on the arches of your feet and allow your essence energy to flow up into your pelvic cradle. At the same time, pull your essence energy into the back of the crown of your head and down into your pelvic cradle. Allow earth and cosmic energies to mix in your pelvic cradle and go up the back of your spine and out the crown of your head. Run your energy for five to ten minutes before you go on.
5. Pull all of your conscious awareness into the exact geographical center of your own head. Here, you will find your soul consciousness. It will appear to you as a bluish white light. Notice your mental image screen in front of your position in the center of your head. This screen is totally permeable and see-through and has a grounding cord of its own.
6. On your screen, visualize an image of yourself and an image of someone you live with or physically see almost every day. Now, watch the cords as they hook up between you. Which chakras are connected with communication cords? Use the cord chart to translate your cords.
7. Drain the images from your screen and allow the screen to retract down its own grounding cord.
8. End the exercise.

Spiritual Guidance
by Lynda Loss Caesara

My opening up was not a single dramatic event. Rather, it was and is a process made up of a series of events, some more important than others and all of them crucial to the process. I was not obviously psychic as a child. My family had good intuition, which was honored if not always trusted. My gut-level feelings were strong, and I had a strong sensitivity to other people's emotions. Everyone in my family did. I assumed it was normal. Later, at Heartsong, I learned that clairsentience, or sensitivity to other people's emotions, is actually a psychic skill and can be used, controlled, and developed.

Meanwhile, my "skill" influenced my life in ways I didn't realize. I discovered that I was good with my hands. People liked me to touch and massage them. I had an intuitive feel for what felt good. I craved physical contact and sensual things.

People started asking me to massage them, and by the time I was in college, I was hooked. As part of a school project, I traveled to Mexico, where I met a *huesero* (bone man) named Don Fidel Ruiz López who allowed me to watch him work. For six months, I went to his house every afternoon. Whenever he had a client, I would watch his treatment. When he didn't have clients, I would sit at a small table and chair in his courtyard studying "the book." The book was a lengthy tome on early physical therapy techniques, which was handed down from *huesero* to *huesero*. With my almost nonexistent Spanish, it took me three months to translate enough of the book to realize that Don Fidel was essentially illiterate and that what he practiced had nothing to do with "the book."

Don Fidel's practice consisted of cupping, some manipulative movements, massage, herbal preparations, suturing, and bone setting. He made clear to me that, as a *huesero*, he treated only external injuries. Female problems, internal systemic imbalances, and psychological problems were handled by people trained in those disciplines.

Don Fidel was a respected man of the *barrio*, or neighborhood.

He had a small weaving business in his home, and I gathered that he owned some land. His family and a few paid workers would dye yarn with indigo and weave it into cloth on two large looms. The clackety clack of the shuttles and looms was a constant background sound throughout the house.

Don Fidel had apprenticed with his uncle, a famous *huesero* who he said lectured throughout Mexico. Don Fidel's clients with both Indian and Latino. Each paid a nominal fee. One confided to me that the reason people came to Don Fidel was that the doctors amputated too often.

I learned an important lesson from Don Fidel, one which has been reinforced by every good teacher I have encountered since. I learned that a health practice and spirituality are inextricably linked. Don Fidel's workroom consisted of a bed and a table on one side, and an altar on the other. He would pray for guidance before working with difficult clients. If he came away from his prayers with the assurance that he could help them, he would work with them. If he didn't feel that assurance after his prayers, he would regretfully tell them that he couldn't help them and that they should see someone else.

When I returned to college, I practiced what I had learned on everyone who would let me, I changed my college major to general studies, and I resolved to study massage.

While still in college, I read an obscure article that discussed the ending of the present age. The article said that the only people who were going to survive were those who raised their vibrational levels sufficiently. I didn't know what vibrational level meant, but I knew that I wanted to survive. So I made the commitment that I was going to be one of the survivors. Later, after I learned about the power of emotionally directed thought, I realized how much that decision has affected my present life.

After college, I felt compelled to move to California. Every time I considered staying in Florida, I felt like crying. So with four hundred dollars in my pocket, I traveled and hitched my way to California with a friend. After an eventful summer and a series of strangely serendipitous events, I attended massage school and found my bodywork teacher of the next eight years, a man named Lauren Berry, who worked with structural alignment.

Shortly after I started my massage practice, some of my clients started saying that they saw lights and colors around my hands as I worked. I found this extremely disconcerting. I didn't like anyone seeing things I didn't understand, especially concerning me.

I had heard that there was a psychic school in Berkeley called the Berkeley Psychic Institute. Within the month, I was enrolled in their weekly beginning classes. After a year of beginning classes, I was ready to start more advanced training. I met Rick Stevens, who informed me that he and his wife Petey were starting a psychic school of their own. I liked their proposal, so, in the summer of 1976, I started Heartsong's in-depth program as their first student.

At Heartsong, my opening process accelerated. I learned that as unpsychic as I felt I was—I didn't see or hear things—I was actually quite adept as a clairsentient. My sensitivity to emotional fields was indeed psychic, and I had been developing my sensitivity through my massage work.

As I began studying emotional fields, I found out how real they actually were and how much I could be affected by them. One evening, I came home from class in a great mood. Class had been fun, and I was excited about all of the new things I was learning. I walked in the door, greeted my partner, and within a few minutes, I had tears running down my face. I knew that I was feeling great, even though I was crying. I realized that my partner had been unable to express his own sadness; when I walked into the room, I had unconsciously perceived it and expressed it for him. If I hadn't just learned about this in class, I would have thought that I had just had a sudden, unexplained mood change.

During this same period, I entered a drugstore and passed by a book stand filled with romance novels. I started feeling the romantic, wistful feelings that these books engender. Two seconds before, I had been thinking about a toothbrush. Surprised by my change of focus, I looked up and saw the book stand. I decided to experiment. I found that within two and a half feet of the book stand in every direction, I experienced romantic, wistful feelings. Beyond two and a half feet out, I was out of range and didn't feel a thing. There literally seemed to be an emotional field surrounding the book stand. I was astonished. If this was true, then I must constantly be affected by other people's emotions all day long, and not even know it. I was quite sobered by the thought. I realized that separating from other people's feelings was a greater task than I had imagined.

Learning how to work with my psychic talent was invaluable. Also significant was developing my relationship with spirits. Don Fidel had certainly shown me how important prayer was in his work. This form of prayer included listening for the return answer. I had grown up Protestant. I was unused to the idea of spirits. In the Protestant tradition, we didn't even have saints. Though I had been active in the church, I hadn't done much praying of any kind. It wasn't my style.

Now, I found myself entertaining the idea that God was a consciousness made up of many consciousnesses, and that each of these consciousnesses could be connected to and communicated with through prayer. A person of practical nature, I decided to work empirically. If prayer worked, whatever the rationale, I would use it.

Near the end of my time at Heartsong came the experience that cemented my belief in prayer and spiritual guidance. No longer a student, I had been teaching there off and on for several years. I was in the midst of leaving a difficult long-term relationship, and I realized that I needed to make some radical changes in myself and the way I related to people.

I started reciting an affirmation prayer several times daily: "I will receive all of the blessings that the universe has to offer me." The prayer was carefully structured. I knew that I needed to learn how to receive. I also knew that I had to stop being selective about the people from whom I received. I often picked people who weren't good at giving and ignored those who actually had gifts to give to me. I decided to stop limiting myself to receiving only from people. If plants and animals had something to offer me, I would receive their gifts as well. I would limit myself to receive blessings. I was determined to stop receiving negative things. I wanted to be able to say no to abuse, in whatever form it disguised itself.

I also made the decision that my next relationship was going to be perfect for me. Either I would have a perfect relationship or I would live alone. I made a list of qualities I wanted in a man. At the end of the list I added: (1) He is perfect for me. (2) He is beyond my wildest dreams. (3) He is better than I ever expected. (4) I receive him when he shows up. (5) I am doing whatever growing I need to do to have such a man in my life. I brought this list to the spirits and sincerely asked their help at least once every day.

The personal growth promise exceeded my expectations. Events happened so fast and were so different from my normal routine that I felt as if I had climbed upon a roller coaster. I felt surrounded by spirits, whom I wryly called my peanut gallery. They offered guidance on everything that was happening in my life. By the time my roller coaster ride was over, I was a firm believer in their existence.

My life became more and more abundant. I acquired a horse, a cat, a trailer, and a place in the hills to live with my horse—all affordable of course. Miracles became commonplace. I rolled my car over in a two-lane road during rush hour and no one was hurt, including me. I felt surrounded by spirits the whole time, and I knew that as part of my growth I had had to be literally turned upside down to free myself of old patterns.

I felt directed to do things I had never considered doing. I attended a ten-day Vipassana retreat. I, who had never sat more than ten minutes in my life, sat ten hours a day for ten days. It was an invaluable experience.

The spirits were constantly guiding and protecting me, though not always in the ways I expected. One time I was forced to apologize to my peanut gallery. My car had been stalling. I did the responsible thing and took it to the mechanic. The mechanic charged me eighty dollars and told me that if the car still wasn't running well I could look forward to several hundred dollars more of repairs. The car was still stalling. I wanted to visit a friend fifty miles away. Not being sure whether the car would make the journey, I asked the spirits if the car would make the drive. They told me it would.

Well, on my way, the car stalled in the middle of a desolate part of a "bad" neighborhood. I sat in the dark, cursing the spirits and hoping that the car would start. Then I noticed two men walking toward me. I sat very still, hoping they wouldn't notice me. Unfortunately, not only did they notice me, they came and asked me what was wrong. They offered to push the car to start it. As they pushed, they asked me to steer it down a side road. Terrified, I replied that I didn't want to go off the main road. They said that they didn't want to get run over. Reluctantly, I acquiesced. Privately, I was giving the spirits hell. When pushing failed, the men opened the engine compartment, found a loose spark plug wire, and the car started. I thanked them very much and drove off. As I continued on my way, I apologized humbly to the spirits. I'm sure they thought it was very funny. They had indeed taken care of me, despite a certain amount of adrenaline on my part.

Around this time, I started studying Christian mysticism and became ordained in an Independent Catholic church. Becoming whole and marrying God, the God within myself, was a crucial step. Ten days later, I met my husband, one and a half years after I started my prayers.

In retrospect, my roller coaster ride wasn't unusual as an opening up process. I moved, had an accident, got turned upside down, had some intense metaphysical experiences, found my life mate, bought a house, got married, and had children. The ride hasn't slowed much in the last few years. Somehow, I don't think it ever will. I've just learned how to handle the pace.

Ritual, spirituality, and a psychic viewpoint have become part of my life. I was not and am not extraordinarily psychic. Everyone I have ever encountered has at least as much innate ability as I do. What has made my life different is that I have spent fifteen years actively developing my talent. Since working with energy is a learnable skill, consistent time and hard work are the main ingredients. I use prayer and affirmation every day. Channeling and energy awareness are a part of my massage and psychic reading work. Periodic ritual (primarily Native American based) helps to keep me tuned in and on track, as well as providing energetic boosts.

My spiritual guidance doesn't come to me in spectacular visions or audible conversations. I usually get a gut feeling that lets me know what I am supposed to do. If I ignore it, it nags at me in the back of my mind until I pay attention, or until the opportunity has passed. Learning to recognize the subtle signals has required some trial and error over the years.

The best thing I can say for having brought psychic awareness, energy, and spirituality into my life is that I'm having a good time living. My life isn't always easy. But it is interesting, very meaningful, and often fun. I'm surrounded by people I love and care for, and I'm never bored.

So, if you are looking for something to change or enrich your life, you might try developing your psychic self. It's well worth the ride.

Energy Dynamics and Interactions

When you were a small child, you observed certain energy dynamics. Your whole house was a stage where you learned methods and styles of communicating, physically as well as psychically. You tend to base all of your adult communication on this original model, continuously reenacting your early family scenario.

Over time, a web of cords and pictures forms that creates habitual patterns of behavior. If you are sending first-chakra "save me" cords that contain pictures of your problems, you are used to expecting others to save you from your own problems. Or you may have cords sending your heart dark, negative "you're no good" pictures that hurt and destroy your self-image. In some families, members learn to shield off one another's cords. For example, a husband may turn a deaf or a shielded ear to his wife. The children of such a couple will grow up throwing fifth-chakra communication cords to people with shielded ears, or they will shield their own ears from communication. Another common dynamic involves sending negative whacks through cords. Energetically resembling a tiny ball of dark energy, a whack is an insult that is meant to light up or bring attention to the receiver's most negative core issues. If you developed the habit, from early childhood programming, of receiving whacks, you will seek out people in your adult life who will be sure to whack you.

These negative patterns of relating can be transformed by changing the way you send and receive your cords of communication as well as the pictures you send or receive through them. To bring about this transformation, you must first return to your childhood and scrutinize the family scenario that affected your programmable baby self.

Family Dynamics Exercise

1. Sit in a comfortable straight-backed chair with your hands and feet separated.
2. Breathe in your essence energy and allow your exhalations to release any energy that is not yours. Breathe in and clean out all body limbs, your complete torso, your head, your chakras, and your aura out to your boundary's edge.
3. Allow your essence energy to form your grounding cord by breathing more of your essence energy into your pelvic cradle. When you have formed a golden ball with a long cord attached to it, let the golden ball drop down into the center of the Earth. You are now grounded.
4. Run your energy, using your own essence energy. Place your attention on the arches of your feet and allow your

essence energy to flow up into your pelvic cradle. At the same time, pull your essence energy into the back of the crown of your head and down into your pelvic cradle. Allow earth and cosmic energies to mix in your pelvic cradle and go up the back of your spine and out the crown of your head. Run your energy for five to ten minutes before you go on.

5. Pull all of your conscious awareness into the exact geographical center of your own head. Here, you will find your soul consciousness. It will appear to you as a bluish white light. Notice your mental image screen in front of your position in the center of your head. This screen is totally permeable and see-through and has a grounding cord of its own.

6. From the center of your head, let yourself walk out into the middle of your screen. Allow your consciousness to move forward through the screen. You will notice a set of stairs. As you walk down the stairs, let go of your present-moment reality. Descend ten stairs. With each step, let go of more and more of your conscious attachment to your present-moment life, and acknowledge that you are going back in time, to when you were a small child. At the bottom of the stairs, you find the door to your childhood bedroom. Open the door and observe yourself and your family. What cords are which people sending to which chakras? What color are the cords? Check later with the chart on cord messages. Do you recognize any of these messages in your family's interactions? Do you see any dark whacks being sent back and forth? Do the auras in your family have fixed boundaries? Or are the auras (realities) enmeshed with one another into one big family aura? What colors are there in your images? What emotions do the images elicit? What words? What do you intrinsically know about yourself from observing the family dynamics of your

early childhood?

7. When you feel complete with the visit to your childhood and have enough information to give you an understanding of your present-moment communication and habits, leave through your bedroom door and return up the set of stairs that leads you back to your present-moment physical body and life experiences. One stair at a time, let go of the past. Step by step, let yourself grow out of those energy dynamics and allow yourself to emerge from the stairwell glowing with your own essence energy, back into the center of your head.

8. End the exercise.

Dysfunctional Family Dynamics
by Judith O'Connor

I create my own reality? How can this possibly by true? How can I accept that what has happened to me is my own creation?

I was numb and unconscious for so long. My environment felt like a storm, the chaotic hurricane of a dysfunctional family. Things seemed fine on the outside. Didn't all people dislike themselves and think that life was hell on Earth? My attitude was negative about so much of what I saw and heard. Externally, I seemed like a perfectly normal member of my family! But my inner child was frozen in fear. She was sexually abused by her father and emotionally abused by almost everyone in her environment. How did I survive the lack of hugs and love from my mother and my father's rough and distorted touch?

To survive I went unconscious, while feeling guilty for just about everything. I so much wanted to be seen and loved, and I thought I had to do something in order to receive this love. I tried to please everyone—then they would like me! My father's control, my mother's fear and unexpressed anger, and my perpetual numbness all contributed to my unconsciousness. I did what I was told, kept quiet most of the time, and hoped that, by some miracle, someone would love, marry me, take care of me, and rescue me from my life. I simply did not understand why I was so unhappy and felt so different from everyone else. Even though I did everything a good person does, I constantly questioned myself. If my father, brother, and grandmother didn't like me, then something must be wrong with me. Was I stupid? Was being a girl really a sign of inferiority? Did God dislike me too? Did God put me here to test me to see how many negative experiences I could handle? I learned to believe what others said and silently felt about me. I did not know how to respond to or reject the telepathic thoughts, opinions, and judgments I picked up from others. As a result, I did not like myself, and I saw myself as bothersome, fat, ugly, stupid, worthless, and, most definitely, unlovable. As I grew older, my sadness and anger manifested themselves in my life's dramas.

In October of 1981, my spiritual journey began. I had just recovered from my second divorce, and my inner voice continued to ask, "Why so much drama?" I was a single parent of two (nine-year-old Andrea and twelve-year-old Stephanie), striving to understand life. All my fears surfaced. What next? Why me?

I met my first teacher, Pat Choat, the Sunday after my husband moved out. We met by telephone. Pat had advertised support groups in a local newspaper. When I called her, I discovered she lived directly across the street from me. Coincidence? I have learned there's no such thing! Pat introduced me to the concepts of energy and grounding, and to a metaphysical bookstore. Upon entering the bookstore, the book *Mother Wit: A Feminist Guide to Psychic Development* literally fell off the shelf. I didn't have to choose. I had my first power book. Soon after, I joined a problem-solving support group for women, facilitated by Margo Adair, author of *Working Inside Out: Tools for Change*, my second power book. Margo was my second teacher. I learned about running energy, group energy, affirmations, positive visualization, manifestation, and the delight of giving and receiving support.

On New Year's Day 1982, just three months after my spiritual search began, I was blessed with a miracle! I was standing in front of St. Mark's Episcopal Church in Berkeley. As the clouds broke, a double rainbow appeared before me, falling into the church directly behind the cross. That day's sighting was the beginning of my career as a professional photographer. My camera and I captured the special moment, to be reexperienced and enjoyed by many others over the following years. Over five thousand postcards of the double rainbow have been circulated around the planet.

By the spring of 1982, I knew it was time to move on from Margo's support group. I did not know at the time how much remained unresolved inside of me. I only knew the group was no longer appropriate. I blessed Margo and thanked her for all her information and support. I began understanding and owning more of my own power, more of myself, and I was quite amazed to see I truly had a mind and perspective all my own. With Margo, I also learned that two different perspectives do not mean that one person is right and the other wrong. I honor and validate the differentness of each of us.

I continued to be drawn to books and people interested in metaphysics. I read, talked with others, and watched myself become more and more intrigued. I knew I had lived many times before. All of the reading I was doing was new in one sense, because it was the first time I was seeing it in print, yet it all felt so familiar. We are living in what is referred to as the New Age, but it is really the Old Age coming anew. All of the information I was absorbing resonated deep within my soul. I recognized truth. I knew I deserved to be enjoying my life, not struggling so much with it. I meditated daily, trusting that I was indeed more tuned in that I had ever been before. Something yet outside my reach and realm of understanding was getting closer and closer.

While continuing to work with grounding and with meditation, I became more aware of looking for something or someone. I was determined to stay on track, to continue my search, not knowing the details but learning to trust my own process more and more. I believed that my life was shifting. My thirties were very intense—a contested divorce, a move from the East Coast to the West Coast, a second divorce, and the unexpected death of my mother.

I had heard about channeling, and I believed that spirits from the other side did talk through people in physical bodies. For over five years, a group had been meeting in Oakland with a woman who did channeling from the spirit world. I was invited to attend. After a few months, I began noticing dynamics that made me feel quite uncomfortable about the group. People appeared stuck, and some of the participants I began meeting outside the group shared feelings of negativity about life in general. One woman had been in the group for four years and was very unhappy. Not once did I hear that each of us could channel on our own. Not once did I hear that each spirit in a physical body can and does channel. Channeling can be as simple as getting answers to one's prayers or as complex as leaving the body to allow another spirit to enter to communicate. The Oakland group was too intellectual, and I felt it invalidated our uniqueness and our commonality. After I voiced my views, I was not invited back. My political awareness was growing. Politics existed within the spiritual community, too! How could people abuse power? I was growing from a somewhat naive and unknowing little girl into a more worldly woman who was learning through her own experience. But I still questioned what life was truly all about. Who in God's name was I? Why did I have yet another drama to confront? My self-confidence and self-esteem were shattered. I hardly knew who I was or what I was doing. My search continued. I felt alone, alienated, judged, and misjudged. My mind was receiving healing through private meditations and my physical body was being tended to through my continual study of health and nutrition, but my spirit was being strangled and begging to be seen! I did not have a religious background, so I did not know how to turn to God. My Jewish mother and Irish Catholic father did not provide any religious training. I could decide that when I grew up, they said. If anything, I viewed religion negatively. I saw it as guilt provoking, controlling, and confusing. Deep within my soul, I had always had a strong sense that the sun would shine after the storm. It just seemed that the storm would never end, and I was tired of the roller coaster ride. Finally, I surrendered. I gave up trying to figure it all out. I didn't even want to try to understand anymore. My spirit was in shock, and I desperately wanted peace in my life.

I had heard of the people at the Heartsong Center. They taught classes in psychic awareness and did readings and energy healings. My inner voice encouraged me to visit Heartsong. Just three months after losing my business and income, Heartsong had an open-house party. I met Petey that night. Finally, I was home. Here, the pieces of my puzzle finally came together. All the understanding, support, and love I wanted were there. My spiritual health returned as I reclaimed my soul and celebrated the spirit of who I am, who I have been, and who I will be.

In Heartsong classes I unlocked memories from my childhood that explained much of my behavior, the kind of relationships I drew to me, and the intensity of my experiences. I had been told many times in the four years I had been studying metaphysics that I had a lot of anger locked inside of me. At Heartsong, I felt safe to explore the sources of that unresolved anger. Some of my childhood memories surfaced while I was in trance; others surfaced in dreams. More and more of the pieces of the puzzle were falling in place, and I saw how the experiences of my life continue to form a story. The story is true, the experiences are real, and the process of finding locked-away memories is vital to the healing process.

I was an unwanted child. My father had fallen in love with another woman when I was still in my mother's womb. After my birth, my father was forced to return home. He was very unhappy to leave the woman he loved to be with my mother, my three-year-old brother, and me. My mother did not celebrate my birth either, and my three-year-old brother immediately rejected me. My paternal grandmother rejected me as well; she was frustrated and bitter because she had never conceived the daughter she desired. I learned to dislike myself, to feel guilty and responsible for everyone and everything. I lived with a group of unhappy, frustrated people, and I felt it was up to me to make everyone happy.

Late many nights, while my mother was asleep, my drunken father would visit my bedroom and sexually abuse me. My mother had the use of only one ear, and when this one ear was in the pillow she was unaware of any sound or noise. My father was a large, strong man. It was a big dark secret—no one was to know, least of all me! I was to pretend I was asleep to give him power over me. I learned fast and kept quiet. My secret resulted in my going unconscious. I was always embarrassed about my body and about myself in general.

My mother taught me to love, respect, and please your man to win love in return. How could my mother love this man who was a drunk, who invalidated her and abused me? Nothing made sense to me. After my mother died, it began to make more sense. She, too, had gone unconscious!

So what did all this mean? As I began to recall these childhood memories, and to review many of the relationships I had had with the men in my life, I realized how profoundly my adult life had been affected by those long-buried childhood experiences. I also learned how these experiences had interacted with my psychic abilities.

I am clairsentient. I take in the energy of those around me in order to know what is going on with them. I learned this ability at a very early age because no one communicated clearly in the dysfunctional family of my childhood. Being clairsentient is a useful ability when one can identify and work with it. In my case, however, I took on other people's energy and then thought it was my own. Others called me too intense and neurotic. Given that I was trying to heal my parents, my brother, and anyone else in my presence, this was only natural. In addition to being clairsentient, I am also clairaudient, meaning I telepathically hear the thoughts of others. This helps explain why I disliked myself so much. I was picking up the negative thoughts of those around me.

When a child is not seen, validated, loved, or nurtured, that child will grow up to be an adult who is confused, frustrated, and self-effacing. My opening process has brought me back in touch with my inner child and what her experiences were. I am not here to blame or to judge, only to see, to process, to express, to forgive, and to release as I continue on my journey of opening up.

Your Psychic Opening

Many of you have spontaneously opened during yoga, dance, or weight training, during operations, accidents, drug use, or the experiences of childbirth, Taoist sex, or the death of a loved one. The intense experience builds a sudden bridge between your subconscious and unconscious minds and your conscious, every-day life mind. A new dimension of reality suddenly becomes more available to you. The newly developing psychic goes from unaware to aware, from unconscious to conscious, from closed psychic to opening psychic, seemingly overnight. Yesterday, you didn't experience psychic energy at all; today, you experience every bit of psychic energy. The sudden bridge between different states of consciousness has thrown you, often unexpectedly, into an awareness that may be beyond your understanding.

Others open up slowly, often while on a solitary journey. Their psychic abilities unfold so subtly that they may mistake or confuse their growing spiritual awareness with adulthood and call it maturity. Quietly, they open alone, unaware of the global New Age that is growing around them.

You may have popped open unaware of what was happening to you, or your psychic self may be emerging slowly and unconsciously. Perhaps you are opening consciously as this book recommends, step-by-step, aware of your process and of your own spiritual awakening. You may already be aware that this process is a pathway, a life journey that everyone is on. Some are fortunate enough to embark upon it consciously. You will be one of them!

Ancient shamanic practices speak of the life journey as a process of spirit breaking apart to be reclaimed and reorganized consciously. As a New Age shamanic journey, the psychic opening process takes its seekers through a reorganization of their psyches. As the seeker, you travel throughout your energy body, your entire aura, all of your chakras, your grounding cord, and your channels, only to be confronted with the stuck or traumatically bonded pictures of your childhood and your past lives. If you are this seeker, while opening up the chakra system you will become acquainted with your latent psychic abilities and you will consciously observe yourself process, perceive, and project the energy you are reviewing. You will actually use your psychic abilities while you are developing them.

SPIRITUAL EMERGENCIES

As your psychic senses are awakened and developed, your entire life history is up for review. You look deeper and deeper within, shining light on some of your most negatively charged memories. In this process, you may experience a spiritual emergency. A spiritual emergency happens when you pop open all of a sudden and experience a flood of the energies, auras, chakras, thoughts, and feelings of others. Sudden rushes of strong energy may course along the back of your spine, resulting in sudden jerks in your body, spinal twitches, a burning hot sensation, or even epileptic seizures. This is called a kundalini awakening. Another type of spiritual emergency may occur when you encounter a heavily charged and traumatically bonded picture you have denied in the past. Suddenly, it emerges and you have to deal with it.

The opening process and attendant spiritual emergencies are like a private Armageddon along the opening initiate's journey. No matter how much personal work and growth you have previously done through therapy and bodywork, at ashrams, at schools, or privately, the darkest aspects of your nature are once again up for review. You have worked with these dark aspects before. You have felt them, looked at them, challenged them, yelled at them, forgiven them, and loved them. But up until now you have not processed and filed them. Once you have removed the traumatic charge from your picture memories and understood them with your soul's psychic perspective, they do not control or haunt you ever again. This soul cleansing resembles the religious ritual of baptism, preparing you for the enlightenment of your own soul's self-realization—living in your own light!

THE PURE LIGHT

Remain inspired with desire to reach the higher parts of your nature. Allow this to be your lodestar. You will often need great courage as you face old feelings and memories. Denied and left unresolved, they have been affecting your daily reality with or without your awareness. Each time you release a stuck memory, you are lightening up your auric energy space by releasing the denser, heavier, darker, and slower-moving traumatized energy. Eventually, you will hold only the pure light of your own soul's essence energy. From Armageddon to the Gates of Heaven, the psychic opening journey expands your awareness of everything!

FACING THE LOWER SELF WITH A TEACHER

The fast-paced middle phases of opening up give the opening psychic a bursting rush of awareness. Each new day, the seeker faces pictures and takes greater control, as each ability develops. During this overwhelming period of growth, the seeker often finds a teacher who is a little farther along on the pathway; such a teacher shares experiences and gives guidance. The seeker finds the teacher to be quite magical, because the teacher seems to possess all the keys to the universe. With the teacher's guidance, the seeker awakens the spiritual warrior within, the peaceful warrior who is fully prepared to fight the battle against the lower, darker self. The lower self is the one true villain you will meet during your journey. The lower self is entangled in personal insecurities, self-criticism, personal disclaimers, fear, jealousy, sarcasm, hate, anger, possessiveness, and bigotry.

What is truly magic are not teachers themselves but the psychic/spiritual viewpoint they offer. Teachers teach by their own actions, by their own lives. They show you that each experience is there to offer lessons and tests to encourage greater spiritual awareness. When you master a lesson, you have raised your energy to a higher and lighter vibration. No matter what happens, you can glean a spiritually expansive lesson from it by shedding light. Then, all experiences become breakthroughs. True teachers gently guide seekers into the light of their own soul's essence energy.

Teachers do not necessarily have to be psychics or spiritual teachers per se. For example, you might meet a dance teacher who can assist you to *be* a dancer in the fullest sense of the word. To be anything to the utmost is the achievement of a spiritual state. To walk, talk, look, and act like a dancer with your best and highest potential is a considerable evolution. Your dance teacher could be quite evolved spiritually. She may have no stuck pictures in her energy body. She may be free to develop her dancing. She may be able to teach you how to be free enough of your own pictures to be able to manifest the spiritual dancer within you by challenging your pictures and your lower self.

Your dance teacher may teach you how to deal with others by using inward focus and concentration. In any given situation, she may be able to throw you back onto yourself. With the heart of awakening the spiritual dancer inside of herself as her lodestar, she can inspire you to move along your own pathway with an equally great commitment.

Your dance teacher may seem quite magical, making elegant costumes for you out of scraps of material or manifesting jobs out of thin air. She always directs you again and again into yourself, into the center of your own heart, toward your own power. She encourages your inner light. Always, and on every occasion, she teaches you that your lower self stands in the way of what you really want — to dance from the center of your own soul's highest potential. The only way this is possible is to *be* your own light, *be* your own inspiration, *be* the dancer.

The Law of Manifestation

You create your own reality. Everywhere you go, you carry pictures of your memories, thoughts, emotions, hopes, dreams, fears, and beliefs. Since these pictures are made up of energy, they attract like and complementary energies. You create your own reality by a synthesis of the pictures you carry with you in your aura and by the choices you make. The following case history illustrates this process.

Example. Gretchen was born into a very wealthy family and was raised by nannies and servants. Her parents were always too busy to be with her. Lacking an experience of love, she was unable to develop self-love. She was a pleasant woman, but she attracted friends who either used her or treated her like an object. During a psychic reading, her core picture was discovered. It said, "I'm not lovable. That's why no one is here for me." This picture had been announcing her self-perception, thereby attracting and allowing others to treat her as her parents did. Gretchen was given the choice to keep her picture and continue her reality as it was, or to release the picture, process it, and file it.

Before Gretchen could release this core picture, she needed to go back to revisit her childhood. She needed to rescue her inner child from abandonment. She met her seven-year-old inner child alone in a very big room in a very big house. Her parents were in the solarium with company. She picked up her inner child and carried her downstairs to listen outside the door to the solarium. She heard her parents and their company talking. Both her inner child and her present-time adult heard enough for her to realize that her parents did indeed love her. Much of what they were doing came from a sincere intention of giving her a good life. Their actual behavior showed that they were so busy creating "the good life" for her they had no time to pay attention to her. Gretchen and her inner child gained an understanding that gave her a new perspective. She came out of her childhood regression with a renewed inspiration to clean up her aura so she could attract and create the reality she wanted. She found that visiting the past offered her an opportunity to change her reality by taking full responsibility for her energy. Once she forgave her parents and incorporated more love for herself into her aura, this manifested in her interactions with others. People around her gave her more love. And she was ready and able to receive it.

The process of reality creation is easy. Decide what you want. Fantasize about how it would feel to have it and how it would empower you. Be in affinity with it, communicate with it, imagine it, and know that you can have it! All you need to do is focus your chakras on exactly what you want and need, within the context of the highest good for all, and you will get it. Believe it!

Reality Creation Exercise

1. Sit in a comfortable straight-backed chair with your hands and feet separated.
2. Breathe in your essence energy and allow your exhalations to release any energy that is not yours. Breathe in and clean out all body limbs, your complete torso, your head, your chakras, and your aura out to your boundary's edge.
3. Allow your essence energy to form your grounding cord by breathing more of your essence energy into your pelvic cradle. When you have formed a golden ball with a long cord attached to it, let the golden ball drop down into the center of the Earth. You are now grounded.
4. Run your energy, using your own essence energy. Place your attention on the arches of your feet and allow your essence energy to flow up into your pelvic cradle. At the same time, pull your essence energy into the back of the

crown of your head and down into your pelvic cradle. Allow earth and cosmic energies to mix in your pelvic cradle and go up the back of your spine and out the crown of your head. Run your energy for five to ten minutes before you go on.

5. Pull all of your conscious awareness into the exact geographical center of your own head. Here, you will find your soul consciousness. It will appear to you as a bluish white light. Notice your mental image screen in front of your position in the center of your head. This screen is totally permeable and see-through and has a grounding cord of its own.

6. On your screen, place a picture of a future you want to have. Is it a new car, a lover, a better job, calmer emotions, or spiritual enlightenment? Visualize yourself in that situation you desire. What would you have to be like to let what you want survive in your daily life? What would it feel like to have the car, lover, job, calmer emotions, or spiritual enlightenment you desire? Allow the image to be empowered by framing and grounding the image with your essence energy. Speak to the image and make friends with it. Become quite well acquainted. Ask the image questions, such as, "What do I need to know to have you?" Listen to the image's answers.

7. Take the image and send replicas of it to every cell in your body to create an affinity with what you desire, so that every cell is at one with it. Know that you can have what you want. You are ready to create it now. Take the image on your screen and surround it with a pink heart with wings. Allow the pink heart with wings to fly off of your visual screen and out of your aura into the astral universe. The pink heart is the color and shape of affinity. Your true desire will be attracted to the pink affinity of the heart and will be drawn back to the desire that still rests in every cell of your body. Like energy at-

tracts like, or complementary, energy. A word of warning
here. You get what you create. Use the highest and most
honorable intentions behind what you create so that you
will receive the highest and most honorable realities.

8. End the exercise.

Shape Shifter
by Michele Jamal

Since I was very small, I have had memories of psychic phenomena that have occurred on many levels and have taken many
different forms. Through the years, I have experienced spon-
taneous astral projections. I have been able to read other people's thought forms, auras, and past lives. Even more significant
to me have been experiences in which psychic phenomena have
opened me up to a deeper, subtler relationship not only with
humans, but with extraterrestrials, animals, rocks, trees, and the
myriad forms of life consciousness.

While I was interviewing shaman women for my book *Shape
Shifters: Shaman Women in Contemporary Society,* I entered a
trance state and saw manifestations of psychic phenomena. After
talking to one woman into the wee hours on the phone, I immediately went to bed. As I lay on the pillow and shut my eyes,
I saw the tiny, iridescent, etheric form of a woman with wings
flying into my inner visual field. The vision was followed by
chords of music, which were visually translated into ethereal,
translucent colors.

In Hawaii two years ago, I entered into a living enactment
of my own mythology. It seemed that almost as quickly as I
channeled information, it began to manifest externally on some
level. Regardless of how fantastic the transmission, it became
a reality within days or weeks. I had entered the mythic world
of the devas.

The times when the most psychic energy is activated in my
life seem to be the times when I am in contact with an intrinsic, perhaps unexplored, part of myself that contains a pure, un-

tapped energy source. When phenomena are the most intense, I know that my inner Geiger counter is indicating that the source is very near.

Almost four years ago, a series of experiences occurred that alerted me that I was in the middle of some extraordinary field, and that its significance could only be understood fully by nonordinary means.

My best friend Alexandra was deeply involved in the mysticism of Tibetan Buddhism. And although I had taken refuge in the dharma, I had not studied theory or mystical texts, and I was not a consistent, steadfast practitioner. I was entrenched in the many challenges of being a single mother who had not found an economic niche and who was barely treading water on a survival level. An important function in dharma practice is to clear the mind of obstructions, and to allow clarity to manifest. Sitting and watching my mind was the last thing I wanted to do in a state of agitation. On one particularly difficult day, I took up the vacuum cleaner, as many women have done before me, and put my agitation into creating an immaculate home environment. In the midst of my cleaning storm, I thought about a lama who my good friend trusted completely. Knowing that mind-to-mind communication is very much in the realm of possibility, I focused my intention on contacting him, hoping on some level that by tuning into his frequency I could see my existence from another perspective. Knowing full well that the work of stilling and transforming the mind must take place within, I still laugh at myself for trying to hitch a ride with a lama. Nevertheless, I put out my psychic call with urgency. Within moments, my mind began to swirl as if I were being scanned. There was a whirl of energy inside of me, and I found myself looking around the room as if from a greater height. The atmosphere around me was very lucid, and objects looked clearer and sharper.

By evening I expected "to come down" from the experience, but I found the euphoria had not dissipated. The next morning when I woke up, the altered state of perception was still with me. That evening, I was scheduled to see an Indian music concert with two Buddhist friends, including the one who knew the lama.

Before meeting with them, I experienced some anxiety that I wouldn't be able to appear as my regular self. I went first to Lena's house to give her a ride. As usual, she was bubbly and conversational. Then she stopped midsentence and said, "You seem different." "How?" I asked, feeling the anxiety resurface. "I don't know," she said, "different."

Then we met with Alexandra. Even as I saw her walking toward us, I felt an intensifying magnification of the energy in my head. As she came up to us, I felt the pressure in my third eye become almost unbearable. I could feel myself suddenly slide out of my body, replaced by an enormous presence. Alexandra became very giddy, as did I. Because we were both aware of this powerful energy, we were both affected in an unnerving way. We laughed as if we were intoxicated and had a great private joke. Lena was extremely annoyed, and asked us to either stop it or share the secret. But we couldn't stop. It seemed as if whatever force was affecting me was doubled in Alexandra's presence, and she experienced it as well. At the concert, Lena got up during intermission. I told Alexandra what I had been experiencing since supplicating the lama. "My God," she said. "I can feel his energy. This is extraordinary." The energy, his energy, continued to be transmitted throughout the concert. My usual sensitivity to Indian ragas heightened a hundredfold. I was so deeply in trance, I entered every note. After the concert, the three of us went out for cappuccinos. As I looked down at mine, it looked a mile away. "Oh shit," I muttered. I felt like Alice who had grown ten feet tall. At that comment, Alexandra went into peals of laughter. She seemed to be aware of my perceptions. Lena had really had it at that point. She was not experiencing a contact high. She knew we weren't into drugs, and so she had no idea what was going on. If we had told her, she would have told us we were both crazy.

After a week went by and I still hadn't come down, I really
had to wonder what was going on. Throughout the week, I felt
an intensification of the lama's inner presence. I felt transported
and light, yet confused by the phenomenon, which I couldn't
seem to shut off. I had unusual dreams and visionary experiences that seemed to be integrally linked to an overall theme
that was developing.

In one of the dreams, a messenger came to my door and told
me that my teacher was coming to see me. To confirm that this
was true, strangely enough, I looked in the mirror. In my mir-
rored reflection, I watched my form change within moments
into that of a man. I was wearing the crimson robe of a lama.
In the dream, I recognized the face, although in waking I didn't
remember what it looked like. In the dream, I looked at the face,
and I felt that I had received my confirmation that he was coming.

In another dream, I saw the lama I had petitioned walking
down a hallway corridor. I followed him until he turned a corner and vanished. On the right side of the corridor was a door
that I seemed familiar with. I walked in, confident that this was
the right place. Inside was an old wizened-looking couple. They
were very small and gnomelike. I told them I was looking for
the lama. "Yes," they said, and smiled very sweetly. They pointed
something out to me, and suddenly I fell into a kaleidoscopic
world, where within moments I went from one beautiful realm
to another, and experienced a blissful recognition. "Yes, I know
this place," I said. "I want to stay here."

The episodes of visions and unusual dreams occurred over
a period of two weeks. Within that time, I had my first experience
of seeing someone in vision. One morning, I awakened early
to meditate before dawn, without effort or conflict. I easily
slipped into trance, and sat for maybe a half hour or an hour.
Then, within the darkness, I saw a small form appear. It was
small but wonderfully detailed. A Red Buddha appeared close
in front of me. A profound peacefulness encloaked him, as did

a vibrant red aura. I was entranced by this form, which only lasted a few moments.

Extraordinary experiences continued. One day, I walked up the stairs to my apartment and felt an urgency to take a nap, to sink my head into the pillow as quickly as possible. I have never taken naps, except with high fevers, not even during pregnancy. Even with little sleep, I had never been able to yield to sleep in the daytime. On this particular afternoon, however, my head felt so heavy I didn't think I could support it another moment. My bedroom seemed far away. As soon as I unlocked the door, I went straight to the couch and lay down. Immediately upon shutting my eyes, I felt myself soar out of my body, third eye first. I looked down over deep, sunlit valleys, with large shadows cast on the mountainous terrain in the background. I sailed in my astral body until I came to a large balcony terrace. I landed and looked at a lama standing there. He was flooded with light and an incredible radiance emanated from him. The odd thing was that my focus was on his bare arm, golden from the sunlight, and on his aura. As I looked up to see his face, I was snapped back into my body, and I awakened. As I sat up, I noticed that the heaviness had lifted. I felt refreshed. The vision had happened so quickly. It was yet another experience I had to process. Why the astral flight? Had I been "called" to that place? And if so, why? Who was the lama? I could not assume I knew.

I spent two weeks in this kind of dream time. Then, an unbearable dizziness overcame me. The room began to spin, and I was frightened. I had had a middle ear infection years before and had experienced terrible discomfort. I called the homeopathy clinic in Berkeley; as it was a weekend, they had to page the doctor. He told me that he could place the remedy in a location outside the clinic where I would have no difficulty finding it, and I could pick it up at my convenience. The vertigo was so severe that I was concerned about driving. But I forced myself, driving very cautiously. When I got to the clinic, I was chagrined to find no remedy. I had to drive home, and I still didn't have a treatment for the symptoms that were bothering me.

As I sat in the car thinking this through, I remembered that Heartsong Psychic Institute had a healing clinic open on Saturdays. It was located in Albany, en route home. I had little hope that they could heal a middle ear infection in a half-hour healing session, but I went because I didn't have another immediate solution.

As I sat down and faced the psychic lineup, I soon became aware that one of the psychics, Phil Chan, was really cueing into me. Three of the healers told me that they saw tremendous heat in my head that had to do with past-life initiations and contracts. Phil saw past-life pictures in which I was with a guru in a temple where we practiced fire ceremonies of some kind. The connection between us was very powerful, he said, and has deep significance in this lifetime. He told me it was this guru who was inside my head. He also told me that one of the physical features of the temple was that it was frequently covered with playful monkeys. The last piece of information pulled me in. My friend Alexandra had told me that the lama I had called upon lives in a temple where monkeys often sport outside.

What was most significant to me, however, was that my head finally felt clear and free of dizziness. The intoxicated feeling vanished as the healers pulled the past-life energy out of my head. I had a three-day respite from any phenomena that were out of the ordinary. Then I received a call from Alexandra. "Guess what!" she whispered. "What?" I asked. "He's here," she said. "Who?" I asked. "The red hat lama. And he's hardly ever here. Do you want to see him?"

The confirmation was complete for me at that point. I was on. My meeting with the lama is much more difficult for me to describe than the phenomena that preceded the physical manifestation of a meeting. Let me summarize by saying that there was complete recognition between us. The hypnotic state was in full force while I was in his presence, but the dizziness never returned. Our mind-to-mind exchange was very powerful, and the effect on both of us was very perceptible.

In his teachings, he told us that he is the red hat lama, and the emanation of Amitabha, the Red Buddha. I was in shock with this knowledge, but, at the same time, I felt a deep serenity. It was as if I had already processed this knowledge on some level before he came, so that by the time I met him I had assimilated the energy transmission.

I had a chance to tell him verbally of my vision of the Red Buddha, and he seemed very moved, and said, "Yes! Yes!" as if acknowledging that it was somehow a transmission of himself.

For the future, I do not feel a need to activate similar psychic content, or energy waves, between us. Rather, these experiences have shown me again the powerful content of the psychic world, the significance of which lies in the direction it points. With compassion, a disciplined mind, and spiritual practice, one can attain an effulgent, generous, and transformed mind.

Chapter 5

Ten Ways
to a More Psychic You

Psychic Meditation

All meditation is psychic meditation. Meditation is the act of relaxing and quieting the physical body and mental chatter long enough to focus on the world within. It is a vehicle or bridge into the soul's normally subconscious world of psychic energy perceptions and impressions. The meditator is brought into a state of transcendence, moving from a level of consciousness that is awake, aware, and focused outward toward physical reality, to one with eyes closed and focused inward toward the soul's psychic arena. This is why meditation often evokes a trance state. All it takes is an ever-so-slight shift in attention and focus.

Meditation is quite simple. You have already done it in this book. When you did the previous exercises, you quieted your outside life and went within to examine your inner life. Perhaps you have consciously meditated before, or possibly you have meditated without realizing it because you called it fantasy, imagination, daydreaming or spacing out. Gardeners, athletes, dancers, breast-feeding mothers, artists, and people who have focused intensely on a hobby or job or participated in active sports have all had an experience of meditating. They have transcended themselves and have altered their perceptions and awareness. This book teaches you to meditate consciously, to be aware of what you are doing, to sit down and take full responsibility for what you are already doing. It is truly quite simple.

All of us meditate. The closed psychic calls it thinking and tries to keep it down to a minimum. The dawning psychic calls it daydreaming and is embarrassed by it. The opening psychic is drawn to it but often bewildered. The open psychic chooses to do it actively and purposefully. In their different ways, they are all meditating and observing their own inner psychic world.

New meditators are often afraid of meditation and trance states. But when you follow the correct steps, there is nothing to fear in the psychic realms. I have never seen or known anyone who has experienced the kind of evil that the film and television industries portray. By maintaining good and altruistic thoughts, and with self-love to protect you, you will not encounter overwhelming negativities during meditations.

In the *Egyptian Book of the Dead* and the *Tibetan Book of the Dead,* it is related that at death, when the soul leaves the physical body, it travels through mysterious ethers ruled by monsters, devas, and bodhas, some delightful and others terrifying. New meditators sometimes experience these phenomena when first leaving their bodies. The delightful spirits are personifications of your higher self, of your love and generosity. The monsters are projections of your lower self, of your fears and unresolved pictures. Any fear you experience probably comes from issues you have refused to look at during your life.

By facing these various aspects of themselves and their pasts, meditators travel through their entire auras in a trance state. After they have practiced meditation extensively, there are no longer negativities lurking in unknown corners of their auras. Such meditators have already traveled through their entire auras in trance and nothing is unknown. Because these meditators know themselves so well, and have gone in and out of their bodies on a daily basis during meditation, death feels familiar and has a sense of déjà vu.

The inner knowledge and ability acquired through meditation gives meditators tremendous control over themselves. In India, meditators have long been known to be capable of altering their heartbeats. The same, long-proven techniques of centering, breathing, and focusing that the great gurus and meditators of India have employed can be yours as well. The following ten steps outline these proven techniques and can take you into a deep and completely safe meditative trance for ultimate control of your psychic abilities and of your soul's kingdom within.

I. Center Yourself.

The first key to meditation is to learn to concentrate and focus. To be conscious and aware, you need to center yourself. To center yourself psychically, you must pull your entire soul's focus inward, into one energy center or chakra. The particular chakra you focus on will depend upon your purpose or intention. When you are psychically meditating, analyzing, reading, or just plain thinking, you will be centered in your head. If you are healing yourself or others or if you are visiting a friend, you might want to be centered in your heart chakra. If you are dancing or playing tennis, you are best centered in your power chakra. Choose your chakra of focus accordingly.

Your strength and your soul's ability to manifest itself will make things happen. Your ability to be loving, to paint a picture, to build a house, or to run a computer depends upon your ability to be centered and in the present moment. Through centering, you will gain an uncanny awareness of what is going on around you and within you; all of your consciousness will be concentrated in one place, not scattered all over the universe, or distracted onto the past or future.

Centering Exercise

1. Sit in a straight-backed chair with your feet apart and your eyes closed. Touch the fingers of one hand lightly against the fingers of your other hand. Then, rest your hands on your lap. This will close off your electromagnetic circuits from receiving and will help you center.
2. Allow yourself to let go of the external world and tune in

to your inner psychic world.

3. Put all of your attention on your first chakra; let all of your ideas, thoughts, and sensations be in the base of your spine and centered in your first chakra, your survival chakra. Inhale and exhale, bringing all attention points into your first chakra. Keep breathing into that center. Inhale and exhale again and again, until you get an extremely clear sense of what it is like to be centered in your first chakra. Two to five minutes will be enough.

4. Gently move your center of focus up to your second chakra, your emotional chakra. Bring all of your thoughts, feelings, and ideas, all of your consciousness, into the center of your abdomen. Bring your entire attention into the center of your second chakra. Inhale and exhale, inhale and exhale, breathing your attention into the exact center point of your abdomen. Keep inhaling and exhaling as you experience centering in your second chakra for from two to five minutes.

5. Now move your consciousness up to your third chakra, your power chakra, about three fingers above your navel. Inhale into that center, exhale out all tensions and then inhale again, bringing your entire focus and consciousness into the center of your third chakra. Continue to inhale and exhale, bringing all of your thoughts and feelings, all of your ideas, and all of your consciousness into your third chakra, spending from two to five minutes.

6. Repeat this process for each chakra, bringing all of your senses, all of your awareness, and all of your perceptions into each chakra center in turn. Do this with your fourth chakra, the chakra of love and affinity in the center of your chest; with your fifth chakra, the communication chakra at the center of your throat; with your sixth chakra, the vision chakra at the center of your forehead; and with your seventh chakra, the chakra of knowingness

located at the center of the crown of your head.

7. Which center do you like best? Play with centering in that chakra for a while in trance and later out of trance. When you do sports, experiment with your different centers. And, when you relate to people and when you work, shift your attention from one center to another to discover which is best for you. Which empowers you? When? Which feels most comfortable and at what times?

8. End the exercise.

II. Breathe In, Clean Out.

Once centered, the conscious meditator can use breath to clean out. All meditation brings you within. If you are opening up to yourself, then your main goal is to know who you are and to process your own self-identity. To breathe in and clean out, simply breathe your essence energy through your body parts as you have already done in Chapter 3. This time, pay close attention to spacing your breathing evenly, giving yourself as much time in between breaths as in the breaths themselves. Inhale and exhale, evenly and in a connected fashion, until you have filled up your body with your own soul's essence energy.

Breathe In, Clean Out Exercise

1. Sit in a comfortable straight-backed chair, with your hands and feet separated, centered in your heart.

2. Breathe your own essence energy into your legs and exhale all energies that are not yours. Continue to fill your legs with your own essence energy and breathe out all other energy. Breathe yourself into your lower torso, breathing out all others' energies. Breathe into your first chakra, breathing out other people's opinions about survival. Breathe into your second chakra. Breathe out opinions and emotional styles of others. Breathe into your midtorso, breathing out any energy that is not your own. Breathe into your third chakra, breathing out other peo-

ple's ideas about your power. Breathe your essence energy into your upper torso and into your fourth chakra, breathing out all others' opinions and styles of loving. Breathe up into your neck and head, exhaling all others' energy. Breathe into your fifth chakra and breathe out other people's styles of communicating and opinions about how and when you should communicate. Breathe into your sixth chakra and release with your exhalation all others' images and visions about you. Breathe into your crown chakra and release with your exhalation other people's doubts and ideas about your knowingness. Breathe into your arms and hands, exhaling other people's opinions about your creativity and about your reaching out into the world. Allow your breaths to expand your energy out past your physical body and into your aura. Exhale all experiences and energy belonging to others. Breathe into your boundary your soul's pure essence energy and exhale all others' opinions and beliefs concerning where you end and the rest of the world begins.

3. End the exercise.

III. Ground.

In order to commit yourself into this present moment, right here, right now, you need a stable grounding cord. Sometimes, first-time meditators fear losing themselves and their bodies while out of their bodies. Your grounding cord will maintain an attention point in your present reality and body. To meditate and eventually to develop your psychic abilities in the physical world, you need to be firmly rooted in the planet Earth. Your grounding cord will reflect a strong commitment to who you are and will offer you a way to release who you are not. The ability to release the thoughts and opinions of others, as well as to let go of any personal problems or thoughts that may be clouding your vision, feelings, or communication, is a natural outcome of a strong grounding cord.

Grounding Exercise

1. Sit in a straight-backed chair with your hands and feet apart.
2. Breathe for a few minutes. Inhale and exhale, filling your aura up with your own essence energy. As your aura fills up, place your attention on the base of your spine. Allow a golden ball of your essence energy to form with a cord attached to it. Let the golden ball and the cord drop as a beam of energy down from the base of your spine through the many layers of soil, rocks, water tables, crystal caves, and molten lava into the center of the Earth's magnetic force to draw your cord in. When the golden ball reaches the center of the Earth, it will fuse into the magnetic core. What body sensations or changes do you notice? Do you feel heavier or more solid? Do you feel a pull at the base of your spine into the core of the Earth?
3. End the exercise.

Practice grounding your energy every day. The more you ground your energy, the better prepared you will be to focus with clarity in your meditation.

IV. Maintain the Integrity of Your Essence Energy.

The whole opening process depends on how well you maintain the integrity of your own energy body. Know yourself! Know who you are: Know which thoughts and feelings are your own and which are not. Learn to distinguish and recognize your own essence energy. Energy is constantly running through your body. The deliberate control of your energy is called "running energy." Honoring your integrity comes from constantly letting go of what you are not, maintaining a clear boundary on your aura, and running your own energy through your channels. A healthy aura is like water. It never loses its integrity, yet it can adapt to any shape or size that contains it. Like water, you can adapt your perceptions and expressions without giving up your soul's integrity.

If you are tired, often confused, frequently sick, or unable to experience your emotions or express your power, then you are not running your energy correctly through your body. When you are running your energy in the correct direction, with appropriate energy patterns, you can fulfill your full potential in any given situation because you will be exhibiting the greatest respect for your personal integrity, freedom, and autonomy.

The Running Energy Exercise from Chapter 3 is repeated here because of its importance in helping you maintain the integrity of your essence energy. When you do this exercise, focus at first on your essence energy color, which describes the intent of your soul's essence. Then experiment with other tones or colors of energy. These tones of energy are also your own essence energy, expressing itself differently. Discover the different forms your energy can take and still maintain its integrity.

Running Energy Exercise II

1. Sit in a straight-backed chair with your hands and feet apart.
2. Breathe for a few minutes. Inhale and exhale, filling your aura up with your own essence energy. As your aura fills up, place your attention on the base of your spine. Allow a golden ball of your essence energy to form with a cord attached to it. Let the golden ball and the cord drop as a beam of energy down from the base of your spine through the many layers of soil, rocks, water tables, crystal caves, and molten lava into the center of the Earth's gravitational core. Allow the gravity of the Earth's magnetic force to draw your cord in. When the golden ball reaches the center of the Earth, it will fuse into the magnetic core. What body sensations or changes do you notice? Do you feel heavier or more solid? Do you feel a pull at the base of your spine into the core of the Earth?
3. Without removing your grounding cord, place your atten-

tion on the arches of your feet and bring a pink energy
from the Earth into your feet openings. Allow this
energy to travel up your leg channels and into your
pelvic cradle. Hold the earth energy there for a moment.
4. Now place your attention on the crown of your head.
Bring blue energy from the Cosmos into the back of the
crown of your head. Pull the energy down the outer part
of the spine of your back and into your pelvic cradle.
5. Combine, balance, and blend the earth and cosmic energies in your pelvic cradle. Allow the mixture of energies
to run up the front part of the spine of your back and
out the crown of your head. Allow the energy to flow
through you. Bring the earth energy into your feet and
up your legs. Bring the cosmic energy into the crown of
your head and down the back of your spine, and mix
these energies in your pelvic cradle. Run your energy up
the front of your spine and out the crown of your head.
Allow yourself to flow with the current of the Universe.
Notice how you get your energy information. Do you
know it, see it, hear it, or feel it? What impressions and
perceptions are you noticing? Maintain this energy flow
for ten minutes.
6. Open your eyes when you are done. Now you are connected with your own source of soul essence energy, and
you are grounded on the planet Earth. Anytime,
anyplace, you can renew and refresh yourself by grounding and running your energy.
7. End the exercise.

V. Set a Clear Intent of Purpose.

The seasoned meditator has an active reason or purpose in
mind when meditating and sets a clear intent of purpose. When
you know why you are meditating and what you are looking for,
it is easier to find your own answers. The more exact your question, the more exact the answer. The clarity of your intent is

very important. Figure out what you want each time you meditate and allow the intent to be in every cell in your body. Postulate that it will be there. Think of yourself as a crystal radio and simply turn to the channel. When every cell in your body is consciously focused on your question or intent, the Law of Attraction—like energy attracts like, or complementary, energy—allows your intent to give you what you are seeking. Totally selfish (against your potential physical, mental, and spiritual growth) or immoral purposes and goals will attract low, negative, and antievolutionary (*against* your potential physical, mental, and spiritual growth) psychic experiences. Likewise, high-minded purposes and goals will attract high, worthy, and pro-evolutionary (*for* your potential physical, mental, and spiritual growth) psychic experiences that will help you grow and expand. What is your intent?

Intent of Purpose Exercise

1. Sit in a comfortable straight-backed chair, feet apart, and be in the center of your head.
2. Breathe in, clean out.
3. Ground yourself.
4. Run your essence energy.
5. Postulate that every cell in your body picks up the intent of purpose of this meditation. Feel your intent in every cell in your body. When all your cells agree, you will be radiating your intent of purpose outward, and drawing toward you experiences that will nurture your intent.
6. End the exercise.

VI. Control Your Focus of Attention.

To meditate on psychic energy, you must also control your focus of attention. You have started to do this through your practice of centering, grounding, cleaning out and running your energy, and choosing your intent of purpose. To focus inward is done most easily in a quiet room where you won't be disturbed.

Focus of Attention Exercise

1. Sit in a comfortable straight-backed chair, feet apart, and be in the center of your head, with your eyes closed.
2. Breathe in, clean out.
3. Ground yourself.
4. Run your essence energy.
5. Set your intent of purpose: to strengthen your focus of attention.
6. Open your physical eyes and your third eye in the center of your forehead. With these three eyes, concentrate on a postulated gold dot about six inches in front of your eyes. Keep the attention of your left eye, your right eye, and your third eye all focused on that fourteen-karat gold ball for two to five minutes.
7. Now, close your physical eyes and continue to focus on the gold dot of energy for another two to five minutes.
8. Release the gold dot of energy and allow it to dissolve.
9. End the exercise.

VII. Receive Openly.

The experienced meditator chooses to receive openly the soul's inner world of energy messages. Psychic energy is extremely subtle compared to the density and mass of the physical world's energy vibrations. So you need to be open to very subtle sensations and images.

The practice of openness will also protect you. When you open your chakras, you expand your awareness and perceptions. You allow yourself to understand more about the situations around you. If your boss yells at you, for example, you might unknowingly take this energy into your heart chakra. It would hurt because it does not belong there. You would have made the mistake of taking his comments personally. But if you open your heart chakra, like the iris of a camera, the pain will leave. You will gain compassion, and you will understand that your boss is simply having a hard time himself. You will understand

that you are not the problem. You will open yourself up to
receive the whole situation, not just his anger.

Receiving Openly Exercise

1. Sit in a comfortable straight-backed chair, feet apart, and
   be in the center of your head.
2. Breathe in, clean out.
3. Ground yourself.
4. Run your essence energy.
5. Set your intent of purpose: to open your chakras to
   receive energy information.
6. Focus your attention on the base of your spine. Open
   your first chakra as you would open the petals of a
   flower. Be aware of any information, feelings, words, and
   attitudes that relate to your survival. Do not worry about
   translating the information; simply receive it openly and
   observe it.
7. Place your attention on your abdomen, where your
   second chakra is located. Be open and receptive to any
   information, feelings, words, and attitudes you have
   about your emotions and your sexuality.
8. Repeat the same process with each of your major
   chakras, opening each chakra and receiving whatever information, feelings, words, and attitudes associated with
   that particular chakra. Be aware of issues of power and
   empowerment for your third chakra; love and affinity for
   your fourth chakra; verbal and nonverbal communication
   for your fifth chakra; vision and imagery for your sixth
   chakra; and knowingness for your seventh chakra.
9. Don't try to figure out yet what your experience means.
   Just experience and observe.

VIII. Practice Neutrality.

With wide-open and receptive chakras, the meditator needs
to practice neutrality, having no attachments, no conditions, no

opinions, no ideas, no considerations, no fear, no hate, no judgment, no disgust, no desire, no resistance, no joy, no sympathy,
and no feelings—no attachment of any kind, whether good or
bad. Simply observe the energy from a neutral point. This will
be particularly difficult if you are clairsentient, but, with practice, you will gain a neutrality about the emotions and pictures
you receive during meditation. If you are clairaudient, be careful
to eliminate thoughts of judgment that might influence your
telepathic abilities. If you are clairvoyant, remember that it is
impossible to see clearly through traumatically charged pictures
if your vision is distorted by opinions about the pictures you
are receiving. Simply observe and experience from neutrality.

When your grounding cord is down and clear, you can continuously release any highly charged energy or any areas of
confusion by simply draining them down your grounding cord.
In contrast, a person who is flooded with attachments is quite
controlling of others and has very little self-control.

When you are attached to certain outcomes, you cannot really
help others because you will try to control the situation rather
than really be there for them. Your neutrality toward other people's realities offers them a chance to be themselves without any
judgment on your part about how they should be.

Finally, to be attached to outcomes for yourself prevents you
from being in the present moment. Practicing neutrality will
help you move beyond such attachments.

Neutrality Exercise

1. Sit in a comfortable straight-backed chair, feet apart,
   and be in the center of your head.
2. Breathe in, clean out.
3. Ground yourself.
4. Run your essence energy.
5. Set your intent of purpose: to become aware of your
   attachments.
6. In the center of your head, notice a small bluish white

dot of light. This is you, your consciousness. Now
create a vehicle in which you are going to travel out of
your body. Project a small astral energy body. Imagine
that this astral energy body is made up of light the
color of your essence energy. Think of it as a being
with arms, legs, torso, and head. Or, if you prefer, as
a being with wings. Connect your astral energy body's
silver grounding cord into the spine of your back to
maintain your connection with the present moment.
When your astral energy body is fully formed and
grounded, open your eyes and pick a corner in the
ceiling of the room, the corner where you would like
to be. Then close your eyes again.

7. Now place yourself in that corner. Bring all of your conscious awareness up into the corner. Feel the corner
around you. Take a minute to acclimate yourself, then
look back at your body in the chair. This will be easier
than you think.

8. Notice your aura. Look for any attachments in your
aura. They will show up as small triangles of energy.
These attachments are dogmatic opinions and desires
that you are holding onto. Simply notice, from the objective viewpoint up in the corner, where you hold your
attachments. Which parts of your body are they near?
Which chakras? Take fifteen to twenty minutes to scan
your aura thoroughly.

9. Now, pull your consciousness back into the center of
your head and center yourself there.

10. Back in your body, drain all the triangles you noticed
down your grounding cord, letting go of all attachments.

11. End the exercise.

IX. Trust Your Soul's Pathway.

Your experience is yours and no one else's. Your energy body
is complete as its own private computer, with its own symbolic

language. When you see a psychic image, hear psychic words, or get a strong psychic feeling, this takes place in your psychic body. No one else experiences it for you or with you. Even if others invalidate what you are experiencing psychically, it is still happening and you are still experiencing it. You are on your own pathway.

Each soul enters the Earth's physical reality for its own reasons, with its own destiny as its lodestar. The cycle of life/dying/death/rebirth is like a school for your soul, with dying and rebirth as the doorways between the semesters of life and the vacations of death. During death, your soul understands the whole system, who you were during other semesters (lives), and what situations you must create (i.e., what kinds of parents and family dynamics) to learn your soul's chosen spiritual lessons. These spiritual lessons will lead you to your whole-a-gram, or a whole understanding of yourself. Your education and experience in the physical Earth reality, including all semesters (all lives lived) and all vacations (all deaths experienced) become one whole educational experience. Your personal pathway is your study card, indicating what courses you will take (what parents and life experiences) and what karmic lessons you intend to learn on your way to graduation (the Whole God Spirit). Each repetition of a similar cycle, such as repeatedly choosing to be in an abusive intimate relationship, is a test. You are given free will to choose over and over again whether you will fail such tests, and have to repeat them, or pass them. When you have passed a test, such as finally working through an attachment to abusive relationships, you look at this not as a test passed, but as just another life experience. Possibly you incarnated into an abusive childhood only to repeat this habit in adulthood. This allowed you to test the constant choice between continuing to attract the same abusive situations or moving beyond such situations toward other consciously chosen lessons. Your pathway in this example would be to get closer to the Whole God Spirit through learning the lessons of self-love. When you truly love yourself as the Whole God Spirit already loves you, you have raised your essence energy vibration to the highest parts of yourself. Self-love is only one spiritual attribute in many on the pathway to Whole God Spirit consciousness. The higher and lighter colors on the Color Chart are the vibrations that resonate with your goal. We all want God-consciousness. Now you can travel that pathway with full awareness of what you are doing by trusting the inner psychic perceptions that have led you there.

Life Pathway Exercise

1. Sit in a comfortable straight-backed chair, feet apart, and be in the center of your head.
2. Breathe in, clean out.
3. Ground yourself.
4. Run your essence energy.
5. Set your intent of purpose: to become aware of your life pathway.
6. Create your astral energy body, the form in which you can travel beyond and outside of your physical reality. Establish your astral energy body's silver grounding cord to maintain your connection with the present moment. Begin to move up a set of ten stairs, one at a time, leaving your physical body and reality behind. Take steps one, two, and three. Each step leads you away from who you are today and toward who you are for all time. Take steps four, five, and six. As you move up the stairs, you begin to notice a warm, safe bright light. You can feel the safety of your strong silver cord's connection with the present moment as you are drawn up into that light. Take steps seven, eight, and nine. Then, with step ten, you are within the light. A powerful awareness washes over you. You are within a vast pool of creativity, at the exact geographical center of the Whole God Spirit's head. Some call this center God; others describe it as the place of the creative rings or shared chakras. Before you

and around you are your reasons for incarnating. You see images, hear words, and have feelings about your first incarnation on the planet Earth. You know who you have been and where you are going. As a baby, meditation, trance, and psychic energy were all very natural. Somewhere along the way, you were told that this was just fantasy and a waste of time. Now you are setting out on your path again, still almost a baby, not having been able to develop your psychic self until now. Be gentle and easy with yourself as you would be with a baby. Satisfy your hunger and thirst for knowledge, with love and reverence for your own soul's psychic perceptions. Place an outline of a heart in front of you and allow all the images, words, and feelings to go into it. As they mix and blend together, they are synthesized into a new picture, the picture of your pathway in this lifetime. Observe the picture as if it were a movie. What do you see yourself doing? Listen to the words. What colors do you know, see, hear, or feel? The colors in the picture are the same as the spiritual lessons you are learning to master this lifetime. After you have completed this exercise, you can review the Color Chart in Chapter 3. The tones of the colors will show you how developed the lessons you are here to learn are. Most of the colors on the Color Chart have four tones. Generally, the darkest of these is associated with closed psychics, the next with dawning psychics, the third with opening psychics, and the highest and lightest with open psychics. Open psychics have followed their own pathways and earned their enlightenment.

7. Bring the heart containing the knowledge of your personal pathway into your astral body. Feel it magnetized into your own heart chakra. When this heart is in total affinity and total oneness with your heart chakra, begin to go back down the stairs that lead to your physical

body. Steps ten, nine, and eight. With each step, you
reenter your present reality. Steps seven, six, and five.
You regain your present-moment awareness. Steps four,
three, and two. Finally, take step one into the exact
geographical center of your own head. Welcome home,
Whole Spirit!
8. End the exercise.

X. Let Go, Let Grow, and Let Glow.

This is a favorite Heartsong adage. Always let go of your
meditations. Do not hold onto the experience. If you hold onto
your energy experience, it will follow you around, inhibiting your
growth and your soul's radiance. At the end of every meditation, complete the experience by draining your excess energy
in your chakras down your grounding cord. My son likes to
visualize his chakras as ice cream cones. The ice cream is the
energy that needs to be released, and he lets it melt down his
back channels and through his grounding cord into the center
of the Earth. This exercise can also be helpful when you are
having trouble sleeping.

If you have any images that you are unable to release through
your grounding cord, you may have to treat the stuck energy
the way you would treat a negative or core picture, by projecting it onto your visual screen and then grounding it off of
your visual screen. The act of bringing stuck energy in front
of your sixth chakra gives you clarity and control over the energy.

Letting Go of Energy Exercise

1. Sit in a comfortable straight-backed chair, feet apart, and
   center yourself in your favorite chakra. [If you are trying
   to fall asleep, you may do this exercise lying down in bed.]
2. Breathe in, clean out.
3. Ground yourself.
4. Run your essence energy.
5. Establish your intent of purpose: to let go of excess and

foreign energies.

6. Go through each chakra and drain excess energy out into your spine, and then down through the channels on your back into your grounding cord, and then down into the center of the Earth. Let go of every emotion, thought, and image. Allow all the excess energy to be released down your grounding cord.

7. End the exercise.

Who Am I?
by Petey Stevens

Comet Kahouteck lent an air of excitement and magic to Berkeley's underground schools. It was 1973, and I was twenty-nine, completing my first Saturn Return and absolutely bewildered by what I had experienced in the previous two years. With the birth of Heather, my firstborn, I went from child-woman to woman-mother. Her birth precipitated a spiritual awakening and a time of personal reflection and self-realization.

The aftermath of the 1960s left many of us with questions about the unexplained mind-altering phenomena we had experienced. The 1960s, to me, were a precursor to the spiritual awakening that the birth of my first child gave me. Soon after Heather's birth on 4 October, 1971, I looked into her eyes and saw an essential purity and awareness that I had not expected. I knew that I had created her body and I had done that well, sometimes driving all over New England to find the organic fruits and vegetables that I could not grow in my own backyard garden. But I saw in her eyes a spark of consciousness that I could not take credit for. As I thought to myself, "What a beautiful baby I've created," I heard in my head, as if in answer, "Oh, you think so! I had something to do with my own creation." It was Heather. She looked right through me—through my body and into a deep part of myself that had been buried. Too preoccupied with "being liked" and "surviving" in the physical world, I had forgotten to honor the part of myself that

I had known so well as a child. I cast off the thoughts as coincidence, yet the experience haunted me.

For some reason beyond my comprehension, I always knew
exactly what Heather wanted or needed even before she would
cry. I thought it was body language or woman's intuition. At
the time, I thought little of the fact that I would always go exactly where I was needed, just in the nick of time, to stop Heather
before she chewed on a leaf from a plant or stuck her fingers
in the electric socket. "Coincidences" were a daily occurrence.

I spent hours breast-feeding Heather in quiet devotion. I had
never sat down that long in one place before. Gazing into
Heather's deep blue eyes, I would lose myself in meditation. All
I thought about was loving and nurturing her. She expanded
my awareness beyond my own personal desires and needs into
dedicated service to another. I could barely believe that this
special tiny human was in my arms. Why was she entrusted to me?

At first my breast-feeding meditations gave me basic information about Heather's needs; then, they expanded into information about personal responsibility. Who is Heather? Why
do I love her so much? Why do I feel Heather's emotions so
completely, as if they were mine? Where does she begin, and
where do I leave off? What is the spark of intelligence or essence
that gives her life and feels so familiar to me? What is real and
what is fantasy? Why is my life the way it is? Who is God? What
makes a person spiritual? What is love? What part of a person
is the conscious intelligence? When I say I am, what part of me
says I—my mind, my body? Could it be my soul?

Up until then, I thought my soul was outside of me and at
best I would meet it after death. But I knew something very
profound was happening to me because of Heather. My
meditative "revelations" altered my understanding of reality
forever. This was the beginning of my salvation and of discover-
ing my own soul's pathway.

My meditation lasted long after Heather had gone to sleep.
I would rock her sleeping body until the wee hours of the morn-

ing and receive answers to my questions. I wondered again and again about the question that agonized me, "Who am I and what am I doing on planet Earth?" A voice, quiet and clear, came to me, telling me that I was energy, one spark of energy in the greater co-created Whole God Spirit.

The voice said that the planet Earth is a training ground for souls. Indeed, I did have a soul, divine and immortal yet still quite unknown to me. The voice told me that planet Earth was a sort of university where I would learn to create my own reality and manifest my soul's highest potentials. It informed me that all my past pains and problems were training for my future. Heather's telepathy was a small part of what I could expect. The guiding voice told me to move to Berkeley, where the wings of my spirit would meet the heart of my body.

That first year, I sought out every class I could find about the soul, the energy body, and psychic communication. The classes validated what Heather had taught me. My love for her had given me a desire to grow and to clean up my reality. I needed to accommodate my little Light Child, to be the best I could be for her.

Heather strongly and constantly showed me her soul's essence. She made me reflect on why I wasn't radiating my own soul's true essence as she was. How could I find my essence? I was told during my meditations that classes in clairvoyance could teach me to read the soul's energy body as if it were a book and that reading others would eventually show me my soul's own essence energy. But I couldn't see. I was not clairvoyant, I was clairaudient. And my clairsentience was wide open and out of control. How unfair! I would sit in clairvoyant reading classes where every other student was "seeing" energy. This was very confusing, because the classes were geared to clairvoyants who could visualize, and I could not. After a while, I realized that even though I didn't know how to see energy, I could feel it. I began to use my hands. Soon, my hands could actually feel the psychic energy body.

I began doing psychic readings and read the information contained in other people's energy bodies. Even though I felt the energy, my hands could not distinguish it. I relied on my clairaudience at first. I would hear the information in my head and then repeat it out loud. The more readings I did, the more I began to understand that I was taking on other people's energy, taking in their thoughts, feelings, ideas, judgments, and opinions. My second chakra was wide open, my auric boundaries were not there, and my sixth chakra was blocked. With a wide open second chakra and no boundaries to separate me from the rest of the world, all energies were mingling with mine. Without vision, I was unable to "see" this clearly.

When this process happened with Heather, it was the most obvious to me. I could not separate from her feelings. If she was frustrated, I was frustrated. If she cried, I felt her pain. Separating from her psychically was impossible. Right from the beginning, I was completely affected by her cries. At the exact moment she woke up, the milk would flow in my breasts. When I was worried about money, she would sit and count pennies on the floor. If I was sad, she would cry. What was I doing to her? If I thought about how cute she would look in her little yellow dress, she would put it on.

I needed to learn to separate our auras and recognize, as Kahlil Gibran wrote in *The Prophet,* that she "came through me and not to me." She was a separate individual and divine being with her own energy body and her own reality. She had chosen me to be her mother in this lifetime, just as I had chosen my parents. My psychic opening was no surprise to her. It was part of the plan—a plan I began to understand was my creation as well.

As the sensate awareness grew in the palms of my hands, I taught myself to translate different textures of energy into color and meaningful information. I was like a blind person reading braille. Since my clairvoyance was shut down, I needed my hands to "look" for me. I was a psychometrist. I had the ability to feel an object and know its history; I felt the energy body and knew its history. I still felt cheated. Without clairvoyance, I believed myself to be spiritually inferior to my fellow students. I worked even harder at refining my psychometric reading.

My hands gained their own psychic awareness. I began to feel lumps of energy. Some lumps were scratchy or indistinct, some were hot or cold. I soon learned from the clairvoyants I studied with that these were stuck pictures. Learning to blow away and release the picture memories in my chakras and aura gave me a freedom that enlightened my life. I had not been aware of the images of my father in front of my heart chakra, nor of my mother's opinions near my communication and empowerment chakras. Nor had I realized how attached I was to my pictures. I did not have to see these pictures to blow them up. I felt them. I felt the imprisoning effect that someone else's consideration or opinion had on my soul's pure essence energy communications.

To blow away a restrictive picture, I would simply postulate a heart with wings outside of my aura and place the energy block or picture that restricted my chakra's ability into the heart with wings. Then I would gently blow it away and give it up to powers that were greater than I. Other people's energy would fly back to them, and my stuck energy would enter the Earth to be cleansed and to return to me as I ran my energy. What a gift! I was giving back life-force energy to those whose opinions I had been attached to, and I was cleansing myself at the same time.

During these early years of psychic development, I met and married Rick Stevens. My meditations showed me that our souls were locked into a complicated karmic battle involving several past lives that started centuries ago in Rome and moved into Egypt. Unable to actually "see" the pictures of these past lives, I could only "feel" that Rick owed me three children. I was told during a reading that once, during a lifetime in Rome, Rick had driven recklessly around a corner in his chariot and had run over my three small children, who were playing in the muddy ridges of the road. I came out of my dwelling, saw what had happened, grabbed his shoulders with my hands, shook him, and yelled "Look what you did. You killed my children. You will pay for this. You owe them to me!" The next time I looked into Rick's eyes was in Berkeley in 1973. I wondered if all present partners were soul mates from past lives.

We got married a year later and had Solomon. Solomon's baby years saw another birth, that of a school. By the time 1976 rolled around, I had been a professional psychic for two years and a teacher for one. There wasn't a school on the planet that taught ethics and standards in the way I knew was appropriate at the dawning of a New Age. My life had always been one of service to others; now I had an opportunity to manifest my pathway.

Rick helped me incorporate Heartsong Center for Expanded Perception as a nonprofit religious and educational organization and a church. During the first five years of Heartsong's existence, Rick and I also maintained a home and a growing family. I spent those five years breast-feeding and meditating with Solomon, Sarah, and Cassie. Heartsong was birthed and nurtured with love and with children of the light. What better way to learn than to watch these tiny, magical teachers who were still connected to the source from which we emanate. My psychic opening continued.

I had a lucid dream that depicted ancient Atlantean healers using crystals, sunlight, and vocal tones to heal each other. My interest in healing was necessary. My yearly checkup had revealed a tumor the size of a lemon. I needed to heal it. I was surprised at how attracted I was to Atlantis. Like a faint memory of a favorite childhood place, Atlantis felt familiar to me. Possibly Atlantis was a part of my soul's past. If so, it must have been a very favorite past indeed, because I was consumed with the desire to visit it again.

It had been several months since my dream and its lucid images, yet the feelings I had were as strong as if it had happened yesterday. I entered a warm, sunny room and eagerly anticipated my dream voyage. Flowing before me was "Crystal Heaven," a

configuration of twelve large, double-terminated quartz crystals
lying on a soft pink rug, inviting me to lie within them. After
I made myself comfortable, I began to go into trance, centering, grounding, and breathing deeply for several moments. I
cleaned out my energy channels and my chakras by draining
all excess and foreign energy down my grounding cord into the
center of the Earth. "How perfect is the balance of give and take
within the universe!" I thought to myself. I always knew when
my cleaning out was done because of a sense of completion.
With my grounding cord secured, I placed my attention on
reaffirming a strong silver energy cord between my physical body
and my astral dream body. The silver cord would be a guiding
line back to my physical body.

All I needed now was perfect concentration. Projecting myself astrally was very different from my breast-feeding meditations. I had to focus every cell in my body on the job at hand.
I focused my intent of purpose on creating an open runway from
which my consciousness could project. I focused my attention
on leaving through the crown of my head so I could slide into
a time continuum tunnel and back into the past. I knew exactly
what I wanted to experience: My destination was Atlantis, and
I wanted to arrive moments after the healing I had witnessed
several months ago in my dream. After cleaning out, I found
myself asleep and dreaming.

No one was there! I hoped I had come to the right place. "Why
doubt yourself?" a friendly voice asked me. I turned around, and
there she was, the woman healer I had come to visit. She was
standing in an open doorway with sunlight shining behind her.
The light was so bright, it looked as if she were glowing. I was
so full of questions, I hardly knew where to begin.

"Why don't you begin in here?" she asked as she led me
through the doorway and into a large, bright, open room.

"Hey, you answered me!" I exclaimed. She smiled and winked.
"And you talk to me. How can you talk to me? How can we communicate so clearly with each other in a dream?" I had never

had such a conscious, lucid dream before. Even the first dream was not as alive as this one. "Where am I?" I asked.

She answered, "You are in Atlantis, the concentric circled center of the world."

"Who are you? Why are you here?" I asked.

Her answer surprised me because it was totally unexpected. "Because I *am* you," she replied. At that moment, I felt the two of us merge. This was a new experience for me, but I felt no fear as our personalities became one, for I knew this to be the truth. I became acutely aware of the special relationship I had with this personality. She was my past life. We share the same soul.

Suddenly I was pulled away, snapped back to present reality by calls of "Mommy! Mommy! Mommy!" I heard Sarah's voice and instantly returned to my physical body. "Solomon called me a dummy!" It took me a few seconds to wake up and locate myself in the center of my head. I opened my eyes and looked at Sarah, who was having trouble holding onto her opinion of herself.

"Sarah," I said, "do you think that you are a dummy?"

"No!" she answered, sniffing back her tears.

"Then you know your own truth, and it really doesn't matter what Solomon thinks. Does it?" I asked.

"No, it doesn't!" she said. She looked relieved. She knew that she would not have to carry Solomon's momentary opinion of her for the rest of her life. She skipped out of Crystal Heaven back toward the living room singing, "I'm not a dummy! I'm not a dummy!"

I lay back down in Crystal Heaven and went back into trance. I reestablished my grounding cord and secured my silver cord. The electromagnetic currents between the crystals created a womblike environment, enabling me to return quickly to my sleeping dream state.

The initial shock was over: I accepted this Atlantean woman as part of myself. She told me to enter her body so I could truly experience her reality and perspective. In my Petey body, I always experienced a dry, crisp feeling, Aquarian by nature and clear as a winter's day. As I entered my past-life body I experienced a wet feeling, slippery and elusive, liquid and flowing! "Yikes!" I seemed to be going beyond the physical skin of the body. I could not stay confined in its form.

Then her voice came to me, "Let go. Don't think. Don't reason. These attachments keep you from experiencing me and my Atlantean world. Bring your consciousness and awareness into me, Alta. Your silver cord will save the future form and time for you. You will not lose Petey. Nor will you lose the point in time where you and your children live."

I surrendered myself to Alta and her Atlantean world and instantly became aware of her whole aura. My consciousness was contained by the boundaries of her aura, not by the boundaries of her physical skin. The edges of her aura felt like skin, sensitive to all around it. The aura itself felt as real as the organs of my physical body. The possibilities astounded me! My sphere of influence was so much greater in this Atlantean body. Perhaps I could control and manipulate everything within the auric sphere—chairs, tables, everything. When I expanded the aura, I could control more, because more was contained within Alta's auric space. Alta's aura felt confident and certain of herself, feelings that I did not have at the time as Petey.

I felt empowered, calm, and strong in Alta's body. She spoke to me again, "There is another among us."

Looking around, I saw no one. Then the other spoke, "We are your overself."

It was the voice. The voice from my early opening meditations was here in my dream. The voice continued, "We are Petey, and we are Alta. We are manifestations of your Earth grid, a personal mandala of inner family, whose alchemical totality synthesizes the overself. Your Earth grid forms a whole-a-gram through which our attention is placed in the physical universe. You have begun an eclectic journey, an initiation, little one. You have released energy and completed certain karmas that are the keys to visiting Atlantis, your beginning point in earth form on this planet. Your initiation is one of self-realization, of realizing who you were, are, and will be, a grid of self-knowledge. As you experience yourselves, you will polarize the dualisms of your dichotomies. Become one with your Atlantean self. It is a maiden voyage, the roots of your own heart's song. You must retrieve facets of yourself lost over time. Become one with Alta and one with the others; there are eleven more. As your consciousness expands, your perceptions will begin to rest within us. I leave now and will return when the wings of your spirit meet the heart of your body. You must begin with Alta."

"Alta, is this true?"

"Yes. Let us totally merge in affinity and become one with each other. We will both learn."

I was eager to experiment with Alta's abilities.

I wanted to understand energy and to own Alta's Atlantean auric sphere as thoroughly as Alta did. I remembered the healing I had witnessed in my first dream months ago, when Alta had moved the crystal healing tools without touching them. I became one with Alta. Immediately, I knew that if I wanted to move an object while in Alta's body, I had to include it in Alta's aura. This meant that I would have to stretch my awareness to be totally conscious of that space. I expanded Alta's aura out five feet, and I became intimately aware of the entire area that the aura filled. Noticing a glass of water on a small table next to me, I thought, "How nice a quenching drink of water would taste." Just as the thought left my head, it traveled instantaneously toward the glass of water. An amoebic group of energy sparks wrapped themselves around the glass and lifted it up toward Alta's Atlantean mouth. When the glass moved, I was amazed, then doubtful, which immediately broke the energy pattern. The glass fell to the floor, broke, and splashed water all over Alta's feet. Her voice chirped up, "Thanks dear, nothing like a foot bath!" We both laughed. What a warm feeling it was, laughing with a part of myself. It was the feeling of intimacy within myself that had been missing most of my life.

I wanted my Petey body to be as capable as my Alta body.

My only problem would be the many doubts that my Petey reality held. I would constantly have to cleanse my aura of other people's limiting beliefs and ideas that doubted the expanding nature of human potential.

My intense hunger for healing techniques had been satisfied. I knew now that if I could direct my white blood cells to eat up my tumor, as I had directed Alta's auric energy, I would be healed. Alta believed I could do it, and now I believed I could, too.

I felt done, complete, ripe, and full of Alta. I knew that she was with me now and always would be. I also knew that I could visit this reality at any time, because of the awareness I had gained of my past self. To me, dearest Alta is a very special focus in time.

When I returned to my Petey body, I woke up to an awareness of energy pulsating throughout my energy system. It was the additional energy and heightened vibratory state I had brought back with me: Alta, her knowledge, her awareness, and the many facets of her personality. I opened my eyes and found my three younger children staring at me from outside of Crystal Heaven. "Heather just called," Sarah said, "she will be home for dinner in an hour." My youngest, Cassie, who was three and very sweet said, "You look beautiful Mommy, and I love you!" She flopped herself down on top of me with a big hug and loads of giggles. Sarah and Solomon soon followed. We became a pile of hugs and love inside of Crystal Heaven. I somehow felt that Alta was enjoying my reality as much as I had enjoyed hers!

Later that night, in my meditations, I communicated with my white blood cells, giving them instructions about the location of my tumor. The white blood cells began to eat the tumor. It worked! I could control my body's health. My dream visit with Alta had taught me how! Her abilities were my abilities.

In my waking state, I still could not "see" energy at will. I still mostly felt and heard energy. Those first five years at Heartsong, I could not "see" clairvoyantly. I wanted to experience psychic energy in my waking states as I did in my dream state. One night, I woke up startled and sat up in bed. All around me was an ectoplasmic, shadowy etheric underworld, which I had experienced long before, as a child. I wasn't sure if I was awake or asleep. I looked next to me, where my husband lay sleeping. He was lying on his back, each of his hands holding a golden scepter, his wrists crossed over his heart chakra with the scepters resting on his shoulders, like a pharaoh. As I stared at him, he turned into a mummy. There was a distant cry from the other room. My baby, Cassie, was awake. As I stood up, the astral world of shadowy figues in the dark disappeared. I could think only of Cassie.

During the days that followed, I meditated often. When Cassie napped, I would sit down and return to the room full of shadowy figures that haunted the memories of my childhood and soul. In one of these meditations, I actually "saw" clairvoyantly for the first time. At first I thought that the black in my head was what I did not "see." Then I realized that it actually was what I did "see." In front of my third eye was a large black pyramid, a bookmark in my oversoul's consciousness reminding me to return for reexamination. I was excited about opening my clairvoyance and frightened by what I might have to look at.

I knew that the incident in Rome did not contain the full extent of my karmic ties with Rick; our history began even further back, in Egypt. Most people thought that we were the perfect couple, blessed with the perfect family unit. We cofounded Heartsong and birthed three children together, yet hidden below the surface was a past-life father-daughter power struggle in which I had given power of my existence over to him. He was the authority, and I followed like a subservient daughter. This power struggle began in Egypt, where I was buried alive, only to resurface in the twentieth century in Berkeley, California.

As I meditated more deeply into these past-life memories, I began to witness my inner child, the baby of my oversoul's inner family, as she sank into darkness. The shadowy room I had experienced during my meditation held the fear. I had to return to that room, because it also held the keys to release that fear.

Wondering where I was, my meditations brought me to Egypt and to Nefphsie. Nefphsie was fifteen, and she was walking from the Winged Pharaoh's temple to the pharaoh's death chambers. At the temple, she had overheard that she was one of the pharaoh's unrecognized offspring. Walking to his death chamber, she began to fantasize that he had summoned her to be at his deathbed to grant her recognition, a sort of seal of approval that she was part of his bloodline. I enjoyed her singing as she ran and skipped her way to this momentous occasion.

Nefphsie's song told of her dreams of saving her father's soul as she prepared herself to meet him for the first time. When Nefphsie walked into the pharaoh's chambers, two guards grabbed her. I began to feel a familiar fear; darkness overwhelmed and consumed me. Then fear consumed me. I was no longer Petey observing Nefphsie. I became Nefphsie, bound and pulled down halls and stairs into what looked like a dungeon. It was then I realized I was to be killed, embalmed, and buried with the pharaoh as part of his death party.

Using all my powers of persuasion, I convinced the priest who was to prepare me for death to let me live and to wrap me loosely in mummy's cloth. The priest was to get word to my childhood playmate, whom he knew, and I was sure to be rescued. My friend and I had played in the tomb while it was being built, and we knew every tunnel. I did not realize that the tunnels were to be filled with sand after the pharaoh and his death party were buried.

I lay in the casket. It was dark, and I had very little air. I must have dozed off, because the next thing I knew I was in the tomb. All the horror came back to me. The torches were flickering out, darkness was descending, and there was no way out. I loosened the mummy's wrap from my body. My clairvoyance was lucid. I witnessed the pharaoh's afterdeath: All his fears turned into horrible monsters. It was more than I could bear "looking" at. I closed down my clairvoyance so as not to "see" the monstrous images, and I ran into a small chamber full of golden objects.

I found a statue that I cradled like a baby doll, I placed several pieces of jewelry on myself, and I crouched in the corner. Frozen with fear, I fell asleep and woke up several times before I realized how hungry and thirsty I was. It had been days since I had eaten. There was a dank, mossy smell to the stones. I began to scratch at them with hopes of finding something to eat. Still crouched down, holding my golden "dolly," I found a small mushroom and ate it. Looking back now, I realize that the mushroom must have been poisonous and the cause of my death. As Nefphsie, I was so paralyzed and blinded by fear of the discarnate death dance of the pharaoh and his death party that I did not know when I died. I refused to "look" at my afterdeath, and I wandered though the pyramid and the Egyptian underworld, alone for centuries with the golden doll in my arms and all the gold anyone could ever want, by myself.

To rescue my inner child Nefphsie, I needed expertise that Petey did not possess. I had to call on Alta, with her strength and uncanny insights. She did not like this man's hold on me in either century. She was determined not only to rescue our inner child Nefphsie, but also to release Petey from the karmic ties that recreated Nefphsie's plight with the pharaoh in Petey's relationship with Rick.

Maturity came to Alta, my inner adult. No longer was I a victim being "saved" or "rescued" by other people. I could rescue myself. I was ready for Alta's dignity, and anxious to let go of Nefphsie's bondage. As Nefphsie made her way out of the tomb, Petey began to make her way out into the world. Nefphsie gained her power and life back from the pharaoh and Petey gained her power and life back from Rick—a karmic debt long overdue.

At first, I questioned whether the images and memories of Alta and Nefphsie were "real." I finally decided that it did not matter. What was truly important was the expression and message given in the symbology. In her book *Medicine Woman*, Lynn Andrews talks of retrieving her marriage basket from her feared rival, Red Dog. Whether it is Lynn and Red Dog, Nefphsie and the pharaoh, the same message is received. Both Lynn and I had given our power and dreams away to the men in our lives, and we needed to take the responsibility for creating our own hopes and dreams back into ourselves, our own energy returned to our own auras. My Nefphsie and Alta were at the very most past lives, and at the very least metaphors from my subconscious mind speaking to me. Either way, they were significant.

I began opening up to my soul's inner family while writing and marketing *Opening Up to Your Psychic Self.* I was on the radio or television constantly. A producer named Janice Edwards Jenkins had invited me back to Channel 4 a number of times, so when she moved to Channel 5 it was no surprise to hear from her again. She called and explained that a show was coming up that she wanted me to participate in. I was thrilled, because I loved every opportunity I had to share my work through the medium of television.

Janice and I communicated by phone several times before the taping of the show, which was one week later. During one of our conversations about my segment of the Afternoon Show, she called a preshow rehearsal. We were on the phone for about one hour. My neck and shoulders started to hurt, and I attributed this to holding the phone on one ear for so long. The skin and muscle tissue in my neck felt as if it were laced with sharp bits of gravel. I couldn't sit still. I went to my chiropractor Friday and had a professional massage Saturday to no avail. The pain and discomfort were getting worse. I became extremely restless.

After dinner Saturday night, my agitation grew to a point where I couldn't stand it. I had reached my threshold for tolerating the pain. The prickling tension became so bad I had to send my children to bed. The urgency with which I needed privacy and stillness grew.

The children seemed to understand this and were all in bed within moments. I went into the living room, turned off all the lights, lay down on the couch, and prepared to clean out the

excess tension in my body. As I lay down, I felt a surge of in-
creased agitation and quickly placed a tiny grounding cord from
each cell of my body to drain out the unneeded and very unwanted energy.

As if in a single moment, the entire house became still and
quiet. Everything in the darkened living room began to fade,
and a bright light began to show itself in front of my piano. This
ectoplasmic light grew until it had formed a Light Being. Somehow I knew that she was feminine, though she was not of
this dimension. Her body was all light and almost see-through.
Her face was pear-shaped and shone like a glistening diamond.
The radiating brilliance drifted over to me as it began to fill up
the room.

I had never seen anything like this before. At first I assumed
that I was dead and that she was the Angel of Death who would
help me through dimensions. The phone rang; although I ignored answering it, my stillness left and so did my Light Being.
It took me several seconds to readjust my energy and reground
every cell in my body. As my energy began to rebalance, she
reappeared in the same place as before, radiating her lovely pinks,
silvers, whites, and golds into the room. As her energy reached
me, it enveloped me. I felt the strongest love I have ever felt
for anyone else. It was similar to the immediate bond of love
that presented itself when each of my four children was born.
Her vibration was love, pure and simple.

She did not speak, but I knew what she said through reading
the energy that radiated toward me. She had beamed down from
a spaceship that had traveled through a time tunnel into 1987.
When I asked her name, she put her finger up and an imprinted
pattern of energy came out of her finger and toward me. It looked
exactly the way the veins of a live leaf would look through a
microscope — millions of sparks of energy moving in the pattern
of leaf veins. I called her Leafveina.

What should I expect from this? Who was she? Was she a
part of me? If so, from where and when? She began to fade out.

As I fell asleep, I could still feel her warmth inside me. She loved me. Whoever she was, she loved me.

My first thoughts in the morning were about the upcoming television show. Past-life integration with Alta and Nefphsie was a breeze, but what was last night all about? I received Leafveina's communications through pictures again. She was not there, but her communications were. Leafveina was my inner mother. She came out of the future. She was a future self to me, as I was to Alta. Leafveina's whole mood all the time was pure love. With images, she told me that the pain I had felt when she first came to me were actually psychic hookups being created to allow her entry into my body and reality. I asked her when she would enter me, and her images said she already had.

I felt almost giddy on the way to the taping of the Afternoon Show. I had just witnessed the most unbelievable experience of my life, and I knew that I could not mention it on the show. People were not ready to hear about channeling future lives on major network television. I didn't know what to expect. One time previously, on Channel 4 live, Nefphsie had entered my body and invited the entire West Coast to come on an astral projection that evening, leaving me holding the bag. I didn't want to repeat the experience. I was also nervous about being on television. This time, there were to be other psychics, too, which would mark a first for me. My mind flashed back as I remembered an event that started out as a panel and ended up as a debate at the Whole Life Expo several years previously. Sylvia Brown had presented herself as having a "special gift," and I felt challenged to show the audience of two hundred that they were psychic too. I have a basic ethical difference with many psychics. I do not predict the future because I believe it to be programming. We each create our own realities from the synthesis of our thoughts, beliefs, and choices; therefore, it is unethical for a strong personality, such as a highly developed psychic, to program others by suggesting futures that are already plotted. Sometimes I do read the probable and possible futures of others, but

I always educate them about how to change the present moment to create a more welcomed future. The debate at the Whole Life Expo was fast and exciting. Alta was there for most of it. It was full of humor and tension. It must have been entertaining, because the room filled up as we went on until it packed in over three hundred people. Although it was hard, the debate was enjoyable, but I did not want to repeat it on Channel 5. Alta reminded me that my ultimate dream of a co-created peaceful world community would only come when I could make everyone right and still get my point across. Leafveina must have agreed, because her love glowed within me.

When I arrived at the television studio, Janice came right up to me, apologetically saying, "I know you won't like this, but the show was advertised all day as 'the battle of the psychics.' They expect each of you to predict futures that will come true, and to try to outdo each other."

I look at her and laughed, "They don't understand yet." Janice laughed also—what else could we do! My assignment was changing. Not only did I have to introduce the psychic opening up process as available to all, but I also had to be sure that whatever had been set up by the show would end up conveying truth. The show was fun. There was very little time to share personally. It had been prearranged by the producers that I would take a crystal and use it while vocally toning energy into Ann's heart chakra. The healing began, and Alta toned through my body. Ann was very quiet and receptive, during the entire procedure. After the healing was over, Ross asked, "What did this do for Ann?" With that, Ann jumped over onto his lap and kissed him. It was a great moment, filled with renewed energy, love, and laughter. Alta was within me, and I felt Leafveina's presence.

After the initial interviews with each of us and after my healing with Ann, we three psychics were set up on stools in front of the audience. I dreaded this part. Reading was easy, but predicting went against my ethics; I had to find a way to allow Channel 5 to win with their show while at the same time politely disclaiming future predictions as cast in stone. The two psychics with me were very comfortable limelighting their predictions. The segment went quickly, yet somehow Leafveina was able to draw the camera to me as she shone through me. The show ended with her love and her statement, right into the camera, "Don't believe everything your psychic tells you. You are your own best psychic!" The truth was out.

Therapists speak of rescuing the inner child, but that was only part of the process. I had rescued my inner child Nefphsie, met my adult Alta, and found my inner mother Leafveina. Slowly unfolding within me was an entire inner family of past and future lives, each bringing back a little more of my soul to me. I was living daily in self-realization, as the light of my own life. The question "Who am I?" that had plagued me at the beginning of my opening was answered. I am the God/Goddess of my own universe, my own reality. I am one with the Whole God Spirit. I am a soul, divine and immortal.

Chapter 6

Psychic Sessions

Physical reality is made up of slowly vibrating energy. When you go within to meditate, you are experiencing the faster vibration of psychic energy. You, the soul, are constantly reading this energy to figure out what is going on. You read both physical-energy levels of consciousness as well as psychic-energy levels of consciousness. The physical-energy reality is easy to read because of the vast degree of social agreement. No one is going to fight with you about what is a table or a cat or a chair. No matter what language, these things are these things. A table has legs and a surface you can set things on. It is easy to decode the table's parts and functions. Over time, the same is true of psychic energy. With practice, you will learn to recognize and decode psychic energy symbols and forms with the same ease. Picture by picture, psychics continuously process energy in their individual chakras by surviving with energy in the first chakra; feeling energy emotionally in the second chakra; being empowered by energy in the third chakra; being one with energy in the fourth chakra; communicating, hearing, and speaking with energy in the fifth chakra; seeing energy in the sixth chakra; and knowing energy in the seventh chakra.

Clairsentients feel energy shifts in emotions or sensations, using their second chakra as a sort of radar, reaching out to touch and feel what is going on. This can be confusing. What was that hot feeling that went through my body? What was the pain I felt first in my gut, then in my head? Am I sad or did I pick that emotion up from someone else? More and more as you meditate, you will come to understand the true source of your perceptions. When you know your own soul's truthful essence, you will always be able to separate your emotions and sensations from another's. If you read from the second chakra, your form of analysis and decoding will come at first from past feelings. After you develop more expertise, these sensations and feelings will bring their own meaning. You will be able to identify and decode meaning instantaneously. At first, start with the simplest metaphors for temperature. Hot is active energy. It can indicate degrees of emotional heat from warm to sizzling. Cold is frozen energy, translated as cold or frozen emotions.

If you hear energy and are clairaudient, focus in on the sounds and words you hear in your head. All the thoughts and tones of voice are the energy you are reading and decoding. If questions come up while reading, simply ask to hear the answers. For the full impact of the message, listen to the tone of voice used. You will also be able to hear the emotional charge within the words.

If you are clairvoyant, you read energy pictures by looking at the images, the facial expressions in the images, and the colors of the energy. Review the Color Chart in Chapter 3 to remind yourself what the different colors mean. Facial images and picture symbols, such as the medical sign of two snakes intertwined with wings behind their heads, or the two-finger peace symbol popular in the 1960s, are self-explanatory. Go for the simplest translation of the picture. Simply look at the image. What are you seeing? If you see people, what are they doing? What does it mean to you?

If you simply know energy, your reading experience lacks sensations, words, and images. You know what you know, and that is all there is to it!

Programmability Gauge

Many people are very open to the opinions and pictures of others. These people are easily programmed by the psychic energy they are sent during a session. If you are doing sessions with people who seem to be losing their freedom and autonomy to the pictures you are sending, pull your pictures back and send them only to the edge of your clients' boundaries. This will enable your clients to receive or reject the pictures at will.

At Heartsong, we use a simple visual Programmability Gauge:

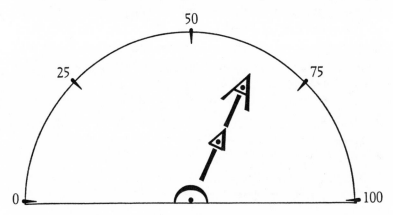

This gauge can be used during sessions and also during personal conversations outside of formal sessions. Simply close your eyes and clairvoyantly look at the gauge. The degrees from 70 to 100 indicate that clients are programmable. The degrees from 0 to 30 indicate how resistant and closed clients are. Clients are just as programmable during resistance, because they are attached to the picture in fighting it off. The region of balance, free will, and autonomy is from 30 to 70. Within this middle region, clients are able to discriminate what is appropriate to believe and what is not.

Heartsong Reading

As you read the symbolic "heartsong" in the following exercise, notice how you receive your information. Do you experience waves of sensations, words, images, and flashes of color, or simply a strong knowingness? Translate your own meanings, extracting them from the feelings, sentences, and images you experience.

As you begin to get to know your psychic self, practice reading from one chakra at a time.

The Heartsong symbol is a simple heart and wings. Clairsentients will feel this symbol, clairaudients will hear it, clairvoyants will see it, and knowers will know it. Place a simple heart with wings outside of your aura and then postulate that it takes on your energy. Next, allow it to shift its shape in front of you.

The main point of a Heartsong reading is how you bring your God/Goddess Self, which is your whole soul consciousness, into your daily life (the wings of the spirit joining the heart of the body). A Heartsong reading consists of six parts:

1. Overview
2. Heart
3. Wings
4. Musical Notes
5. Sun, Moon, and Quadrants
6. First or Relevant Past Life

Reading Your Heartsong Exercise

1. Sit in a comfortable straight-backed chair, feet apart, and center yourself in the chakra you want to read from.
2. Breathe in, clean out.
3. Ground yourself.
4. Run your essence energy.
5. Set your intent of purpose: to read your own Heartsong.
6. *Overview.* It is essential to establish an overview for a Heartsong reading, as for all readings, to help you focus on what you are doing. Imagine or fantasize a winged heart outside of your aura. Allow your energy to flow into the winged heart, forming and shaping it. What is your first impression of this symbol? Does it come to you as an image or as a feeling? If the wings are less dominant than the heart, you may be denying your soul's

reality. If the colors of the heart and wings clash, you may be experiencing a war between body and soul. If the colors of the heart and wings are harmonious, there is general peace between your body and your soul. If there is no distinction between heart and wings, if they have melted into one blob of energy, you may need more clarity. If there is a distinct heart with wings of the same color, you may be experiencing your God/Goddess Self, your higher self, in everyday life.

7. **Heart.** The heart represents the body; the established characteristics that are manifested within life. The shape of the heart defines your basic attitudes. Look at the viscosity, balance, fullness, breadth, and color of the heart. The color indicates which color ray you entered this lifetime on—where you started from. This often gives you information on your life lessons, purpose, and pathway.

8. **Wings.** The wings represent your soul essence and the twelve dimensional levels of consciousness of the God/Goddess Self. The attachment and dominance of each feather and its distance from the heart shows the degree of integration of information on each level of consciousness that you have already manifested in your daily life. The Heartsong symbol has six feathers on each side of the heart, and each feather represents one level of consciousness. The color of the wings represents the soul's essence color. If the feathers are all different colors yet attached to the heart, you have integrated your levels of consciousness, although it is still possible you are being influenced by another person's ideas or opinions and confusing them with your own truth. See the Levels of Consciousness Chart for further guidance in interpreting the wings.

(1) Physical (reproduction, physical body)
(2) Emotional (communication, biorhythms, instincts, feelings)
(3) Causal (action, movement)
(4) Intuitive (understanding, inner voice)
(5) Psychological (personality patterns, games, styles, relationships)
(6) Psychic (energy patterns, dreams, imagination, unconscious activity)
(7) Analytical (thought processes)
(8) Spiritual (soul, higher self)
(9) Mathematical (geometric equations, astrology)
(10) Theoretical (plans, probabilities)
(11) Conceptual (original ideas, possibilities)
(12) Whole God Spirit (creation)

9. *Musical Notes.* Musical notes within the heart represent the number of children you have or will have. Musical notes outside of the heart represent creative ventures or projects. To discover the sex (male or female) of a child or the type of creative project, simply open up the musical note as you would a door and read the information you find there.

10. **Sun, Moon, and Quadrants.** The sun, moon, and quadrants represent your spiritual pathway. The sun is the body, and the moon is the soul. Visualize the sun on the right side of the winged heart and the moon on the left. Allow your energy to flow into the sun and moon to position it. The Quadrant Picture will help you read the quadrants. The fourth quadrant represents the soul or body on its own spiritual pathway. God/ Goddess and autonomy are understood personally, ex- periencially, and with certainty. If your sun or moon is in the fourth quadrant, you are on your own pathway. The third quadrant represents the soul or body that is searching for its own pathway and self-knowledge. God/ Goddess is being questioned and investigated. If your sun or moon is in the third quadrant, you are searching for your own pathway. The second quadrant represents the soul or body that is following someone else's belief or an organized religion's belief in God/Goddess. Dogma often lies within this region. If your sun or moon is in the second quadrant, you are following another's path- way. The first quadrant represents the soul or body that believes only in the physical plane. Its stance is: If you can't see it, taste it, or touch it, it isn't real. If your sun or moon is in the first quadrant, you have no pathway.

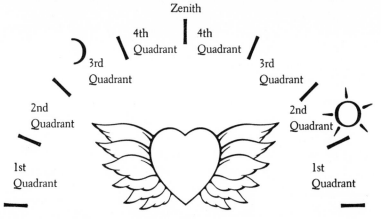

In your quadrant picture, the soul (moon) may be ahead of the sun (body). An example of this would be a moon in the third quadrant and a sun in the second. Our souls are often just ahead of our bodies and ahead of our ability to manifest lessons in the physical realm.

11. *First or Relevant Past Life.* Open the heart as if it were a door. In it, you will find the first or most relevant past life. You will probably get an image of this past life, but sometimes you will simply feel it. Notice the sex, age, location, and life situation of this past self and ask why this particular life came up in the reading. Open yourself to receive any information this past life has to offer you.

12. End the exercise.

Reading Someone Else's Heartsong Exercise

1. Sit opposite your client in a comfortable straight-backed chair, feet apart, and be in the center of your head.
2. Breathe in, clean out.
3. Ground yourself into the center of the Earth.
4. Run your essence energy.
5. Let go of all opinions, pictures, and personal emotions, and ground off any other excess energy.
6. Be in the present moment and commit yourself fully to the reading.
7. Create your boundaries to make a separation between you and your client.
8. Establish neutrality.
9. Make a compassionate heart connection with your client and set a strong intent of sincere purpose.
10. Set up your visual screen and ask for your client's essence energy color to appear. Run your energy at that color. By doing this, you match energy with your client, and you will see what your client's highest essence needs you to see.

11. In your imagination, place the outline of a heart with wings in front of your client and allow your perception of your client's energy to flow into the symbol; let the energy color and shape this symbol. What color does the heart seem to be? How is it shaped? What does the shape mean to you? Are the wings attached to the heart? If not, which levels are not attached? What color or colors are the wings? What does the relationship between the heart and the wings mean to you? Read the musical notes, the sun, moon, and any quadrants, and the first or relevant past life. Do not push your images on the other; allow your client to integrate what fits.

12. Clean out your energy channels.

13. Separate from your client by finding five physical differences between you and your client. Release through your grounding cord all energy that is not yours. Breathing in and cleaning out for ten minutes is the best way to separate your energy from your client's.

14. Let go of the reading and come out of trance.

Sample Heartsong Reading

The following reading is a sample from a Psychic Fair, where readers do anywhere from five to fifteen twenty-minute readings.

Jessie pulled her chair up in front of me.

"Please pull your chair back," I asked. I had already done twelve readings, and my auric space needed room to expand.

"Please wait a minute, Jessie. I need to clean out." I went back into trance and drained out all my chakras, put down my grounding cord, reaffirmed my boundaries, and filled myself up with my own energy. When I do not take those few minutes to clean out and reestablish my energy between readings, I literally carry information from one reading into the next. "Why are you here, Jessie?" I asked.

"I'm here for a Heartsong reading," she returned.

"Please keep your hands and feet apart and be open to, yet

not programmed by, the information given during the reading.
Take what feels right and throw away any other information,"
I suggested.

I closed my eyes again. Jessie sat before me. I placed an outline
of a heart with wings between our auras and watched her energy
fill up and shape the Heartsong.

OVERVIEW

"Let me first describe the heart and wings I see. Both are
plump and full, with the heart a little larger. All of the wings
on the right side are folded over the heart. The heart has cartoon eyes, and the right wings are covering the right eye. The
heart is a peach color, and the wings are a light orange. Because
the heart is a little larger, it shows that your physical body's reality
is more real to you than your soul's and that you spend more
time and energy on physical matters than on spiritual matters.
It is interesting that the wings are folded over. I wonder what's
behind those wings. The cartoon face looks happy, but I have
a feeling that is not the whole truth. Let me pull these wings
back. Ah, just as I suspected. The other cartoon eye is crying."

I questioned my inner voice to determine where Jessie's sadness came from. I repeated the answer I heard, "Jessie, you married a man for your parents and not for yourself. The half of
you that is happy is the part that loves having children and being
a mother. The part of you that is sad is the part that feels trapped
in your marriage.

"The orange and peach colors are very similar in tones and
have a warm feeling about them, which is a telltale sign that
you are quite close to experiencing your higher self, but until
the wings are extended out, your higher self will only visit and
not take up permanent residence."

HEART

I continued reading Jessie's heart: "Your body's reality is more
dominant than your soul's reality because, without a happy, func-

tional marriage, you are preoccupied with healing that part of your life and have little time left to develop an expanded spiritual awareness. You are very hung up on what others think of you. This is why you are hiding your sad eye; you want to keep up appearances. But behind those appearances is a very real sadness. You are tormented about breaking up your family by divorce, yet you are totally unhappy with the older man you married. You fear what your mother might say. You fear hurting your children, and you fear taking care of yourself and your children alone. These fear pictures are coming out of the sad cartoon eye on your heartsong. The peach color of the heart suggests a nurturing personality. But the eye is a dark purple, which represents the fixed opinions, or dogma, you have taken on about marriage and divorce. You are nurturing to others, yet you do not always fulfill your own needs. Often the conflict between what other people want and what society expects of you makes you unhappy. Your life's lesson is to learn to nurture yourself as well as others.

"The plump full heart tells me that even though you are try-ing to please others, you still do everything with gusto, full and rich. That is why your hidden unhappiness is so destructive to you. It is felt and hidden by your gusto. If there are emotions to be felt, you feel them with verve.

"You are very quiet, Jessie. Is the pace and depth of content comfortable for you?" I asked.

"Yes," she returned, "but I didn't expect to be seen so quickly."

"Do you want me to stop?" I questioned.

"No, please go on," she answered, "I'm just surprised."

WINGS

I continued: "The wings are smaller than your heart, but still rich and full. The wings are the different parts of your soul's higher and more consciously expanded self. You do not place

as much attention on your spiritual growth as you do your physical existence; yet when you do place attention on your spiritual
self, you give it the same full gusto that you've given to your
physical life. The levels of your soul's consciousness are repre-
sented on the left side of your heartsong. You are open to the
physical, causal, psychological, analytical, mathematical, and conceptual levels of consciousness. You hide behind the levels of
consciousness on the right side, the emotional, intuitive, psychic,
spiritual, theoretical, and Whole God Spirit, which you have yet
to develop. Part of the mismatch in your marriage, besides the
marriage itself, which was a way to get your own mother's approval, comes from the use of your more emotional and psychic
self. You hide your sadness and pain behind an underdeveloped
set of consciousness levels. You have so much fear of dogma
and judgment. It is very difficult for you to peek out from behind
your wings to feel like a free and open woman. It seems a psychic
battle is going on. Your husband is controlling you through your
underdeveloped, immature levels of consciousness. With the vast
age difference of eighteen years that I am seeing, you were more
of a daughter to him at the beginning. You have outgrown that
childlike mode of behavior, but he hasn't. He expects you to
act like an emotional and needy little girl. To please him, you
do, yet you do not please yourself.

"Coming out of the purple eye in the heart is a picture show-
ing you at age six and a half. You were late to kindergarten and
were sent to the principal's office. You heard him yelling at
another late child, so by the time you got to him you were fear-
ful of getting punished and yelled at. You walked into his big
office, and the minute he opened his mouth you started to cry.
Your tears melted his heart, and he did not yell at you. From
then on, you used your emotions and psychic flashes for self-
protection rather than spiritual development. This experience
also set a picture pattern of reacting emotionally when someone
is picking on you. You figure the pattern worked before, why
not now?

"Quite honestly, it is as if all the more sensitive parts of your psychic nature are used to manipulate or deflect away pain and hurtful situations. This is dysfunctional behavior. Emotions and psychic senses are more functionally used to communicate and express yourself. This is what would be happening if the wings were all open and extended outwardly."

MUSICAL NOTES

"There are three musical notes in your heartsong and one almost shadowlike note. Two are directly within the heart and represent your two sons. The musical note outside of the heart represents a creative project. When I open the note, many other notes come out. The stems on the notes are paintbrushes, and each little note contains an oil painting. Your life's main creative project is to be a prolific oil painter."

Jessie stopped me, "Does it show the baby girl I lost at birth two years ago?"

"That was the shadow note I saw. Your lost baby was an experience in letting go for you, and an experience in feeling a body for the young soul who created it. But the soul was quite new to this universe and did not know how to run a body or build one. In fact, there was no interest. If there had been an autopsy, it would have disclosed that your baby was severely handicapped and death inevitable."

"You're right. There was an autopsy, and she was severely handicapped," Jessie said with amazement.

SUN

"Your sun has just come out of the second quadrant and into the third quadrant. You are just beginning to search for your own pathway. The art you have been doing the past three years has a lot to do with the beginning of your search."

MOON

"Your moon has come to the end of searching. It is almost

at the end of the third quadrant. Your soul is slightly farther ahead in awareness than your body, as if you know what to do in a given situation, yet cannot always muster up the will to do it. The soul knows, but the body cannot perform."

FIRST OR RELEVANT PAST LIFE

"When I open up the heart, a past life jumps out at me immediately. There you are in the French Revolution, a servant to the royal house. You used all of your abilities to protect your politically rebellious brother and friends. Often you knew of the following day's guillotine list and would be able to warn the others. Of course, you were eventually caught and guillotined yourself. Your present fears of speaking out for yourself and your desire to speak out to save others at your own risk comes from this past life. In this lifetime, you are working at completing this old karmic cycle so that you can speak up for yourself without the risk of losing yourself to the needs of others."

Before leaving, Jessie asked, "Is there any one thing I can do to open up my folded wings?"

"Sure. Bring the dogma out in the light. Look at it. Face it. Meditating is quite helpful because you can literally help yourself open your wings up by visually doing it. Simple, safe, and easy. Picture the heart with wings as it was read today. Then open it up and extend the wings. During your meditation, you will be confronted with the pictures hidden in the purple eye of dogma. As you see them, release them into the center of the Earth. Those that are made out of your energy will return to you as your truth, and those that are made of others' energy will return to them."

Psychic Healing

Whole health can be described as existing when the auric energy is flowing within a constant ebb and flow of movement. Stuck or blocked energy demands that you actively and specifically heal that particular area. Because of its nature, the energy that moves very slowly eventually becomes blocked or stuck enough to manifest on a physical level as a cold, tumor, broken leg, depression, cancer, or even death.

Pain and dis-ease are the physical body's acknowledgment or awakener that your client is out of alignment with his/her particular life purpose or pathway. In this way, an illness can be a communication tool for increasing self-awareness. What is needed must be given on a direct energy level through channeling. As a healing channel, you will always be refining the quality of the energy you channel during healings. Continuous exploration of healing and channeling is a conscious pathway that will eventually lead to the Whole God Spirit.

It is important that you, as healer, respect the client's freedom and autonomy. All healing is self-healing, and it is up to each client to allow the healing energy to enter his/her auric field. You cannot force clients to be healed. It is their responsibility to receive the healing. Your responsibility as healer is to be an open and clear channel for healing energy and a sort of cheerleader to your clients' souls to awaken and cheer on their havingness for the healing. Your ability to truly touch another's soul without taking on the other's energy is a central aspect during the experiential teaching that is happening as you are giving a healing.

Psychic Healing Exercise

1. Stand behind your seated partner.
2. Breathe in, clean out.
3. Ground yourself.
4. Run your essence energy.
5. Set your intent of purpose: to be a clear channel for healing energy.
6. Set up your visual screen so you can observe the healing.

    There is great power in visualizing a healthy bright energy body around your client.

7. Give the healing. Open up your healing channels and *be* an open channel. Run your energy and instead of allowing it to go out your crown center, at your heart center allow the energy to channel down your arms. Place your hands, palms down, over the client's head and channel healing energies through your hands into the crown center. Send the energy down the channels on your client's back and on down the grounding cord, cleaning out debris and foreign energies. Allow the Earth's magnetic pull to work with you as you channel. Allow yourself to "see" the energy channeling. Open up and give of yourself, your entire self focused in the present moment, right here doing the heal-ing. Go through each chakra, starting at the seventh, hooking each chakra up to the channels on the back. Clean out foreign energies and blocks; ease out cords; remove pictures, masks, screens, shields, and whacks; and harmonize and balance each chakra. Clean out arm channels and hand chakras. Then clean out leg chan-nels and feet chakras. Move into the client's aura, clean-ing out all foreign energies by combing through the aura. Create and strengthen the client's boundary so that there is a firm end to the energy body to maintain your client's integrity. To bring closure to the healing, you may place your hands on your client's shoulders and say out loud, "Be one, be whole, be healed."
8. End the healing cleanly.
9. Separate from your client, deenergize matching and stuck pictures, and clean yourself out.
10. Let go of the healing and come out of trance.

Psychic Engineer
by Phil Chan

Ever since I can remember, I have always seen auras. It wasn't until I was in my thirties that I realized other people didn't.

Often, I am able to see people's problems based on the colors in their auras. Once, my in-laws brought their best friends, Al and Mildred, to visit because Mildred had constantly complained of health problems. Looking at her aura, I saw she was physically healthy except for a need for attention. I was not asked to read Al's aura because he was feeling fine, but I could see he had a very serious problem. There was a large gray cloud over his head. I explained what I saw to my in-laws and strongly suggested they encourage Al to get a checkup with a doctor. He had a checkup two weeks later, and his doctor found a tumor in his brain. He died a month later.

As an engineer, I have constantly wondered how psychic phenomena work. I always wanted to have proof and even doubted the facts many times. In one instance seven years ago, my supervisor at Cal Trans, Ralph, came over to my desk and said, "You'll never guess what is in this letter." In my mind, I could see the letter typewritten, and I read it to him. He said, "Oh, so you've already seen the letter?" He was the only person who had read the letter. It was written to him, and he opened it. It was a very unusual letter, different from our regular mail, and it was from a person concerned about engineering whom neither of us knew. Also interesting is that the letter was handwritten and I saw it in my mind as typewritten.

The next evening, my wife and I were invited to the house of Catherine, an acquaintance, to meet a known psychic who had been tested at Duke University. After I arrived, the psychic made me feel very uncomfortable; she kept talking about the spirits flying around the room and asked what I saw. Interestingly enough, I did see an image of my supervisor's wife, who I had only seen twice. Upon leaving, the psychic said what a wonderful aura the host had and didn't I agree. But I didn't agree; I had seen a problem in Catherine's neck at the base of her skull. People were a little upset with me when I left.

The next morning at work, I told my supervisor, Ralph, about seeing the image of his wife at around 8:00 P.M., and Ralph asked if I had gotten the message. What message? Ralph called the night before because his wife wanted to relate what happened to them at dinner out. He had just told his wife about my reading the letter earlier in the day. After they were served soup, his wife had wanted some Tabasco sauce for her soup. A few minutes later, the waiter came from the kitchen with a bottle of Tabasco. Ralph asked the waiter how he knew to bring the Tabasco. The waiter said he was sitting in the kitchen eating his dinner when he felt someone wanted Tabasco sauce. Ralph's wife was so excited that they tried to call me that evening. My supervisor had never before called me in the evening.

A year passed, and my wife received a telephone call from Catherine thanking us for being honest with what I saw in her aura. She did discover a problem with her neck shortly thereafter and had recovered. She just wanted us to know and for me to receive confirmation of what I had seen.

Another year passed. One day, Catherine's image popped into my head, so I decided to call her. She was seriously ill, had had her spleen taken out recently, and could not work. The doctors did not know what the continuing problem was. Catherine asked me to come and read her aura. I saw a mustard yellow color that meant to me that poison was in her system. So I told her, but I did not know how to help and I asked her to continue seeing the doctors.

The following weekend, my wife, Beth, invited me to attend a class with her at Rosebridge University. Beth had been a computer systems analyst for over ten years but had left her job because it was unfulfilling. She was studying psychology. I thought it might be interesting to see what her classes were like. When I arrived, I found the class was entitled "Self-Esteem." I was disappointed, as this was something I didn't think I needed, but the class turned out to be outstanding. It changed my whole life. During the class, Dr. Pecci led us through a meditation. I had not meditated before, and during that meditation a white light passed through my body, making me feel bliss. I had never felt this before, and a voice said to me, "Be a Healer." I felt so good, I began to cry. My tears were joyous; it was as though my soul was touched and I was at one with all things.

That evening at midnight, I meditated again and saw an image of Catherine. There was a gray Z across her heart and abdomen. Then I visualized a bluish white light going all around her body. I called Catherine the next morning and asked how she felt. She said she had gone to bed early the night before, but sometime during her sleep she had felt energized and awoke in the morning feeling better than she had felt for a long time.

I told her what I had done and said I would do it again in the evening. That evening I meditated again, picturing myself in a beautiful, peaceful garden, but this time a beautiful fairy in a multicolored dress took my hand and told me to rest and follow her. She took me up a long spiral staircase, up to just above the clouds; then she told me to let go and play. I went into the clouds doing somersaults, feeling really free as I floated in space. It was wonderful. After a while, the fairy called to me and led me further up the stairs. We reached a beautiful temple with white pillars. In the temple were people with white robes. I didn't recognize anyone. We went through the temple into another chamber, where seated before me was a table and four men. To the left, the first one had a hood over his head and his eyes were full of compassion; the second had a long white beard with curls and looked full of wisdom; the third had a simple, peaceful face; and the last had great strength and the face of a warrior.

Then a strong voice from above said, "Go out and heal my people."

I asked, "Why me? I already have so much to do."

The voice said, "It is your pathway."

I asked more questions, which the voice answered. The voice gave me more insight about my life than I could ever have figured out myself. I came back out of trance, and from that moment on life had a different meaning. I began to do hands-on healings. To my surprise, people got well.

I was very unsure of myself. Beth asked around her school and someone suggested I check out Heartsong. Beth and I attended a Friday night discussion, and I felt right at home. I joined immediately and went through the entire psychic development program.

I will always remember my first reading with the public. Jay, a Heartsong teacher, said this was a very unusual request and to do the best I could. I looked at the man I was being introduced to and saw an image of a red 1965 Mustang in beautiful condition with a body of blue water in the background. I explained what I saw, and he said, "I came to ask if I should spend the time and money to go to Salt Lake City to check out a white 1964 Mustang that was in an ad." He was worried about rust.

I told him, "No, you'll find the car you want in the Bay Area, near a body of fresh blue water. The name Benicia comes to mind."

My confidence also grew following a couple's reading I did. I started to describe all the spirits I saw around their auras. I said to myself, "You're really going down the deep end with this wild reading." After the reading I told the couple that I would remove the spirits in the healing room, and they asked if they could show me some pictures before I did. I thought that was weird and wondered what they wanted to show me. They showed me some pictures taken with Kirlian photography, and in the pictures was everything I had described to them. About fifteen people in the school at that time also shared the pictures. This constant validation and the sharing of knowledge continues to foster my growth and opens me up to new levels.

Crystal Heaven

Crystal Heaven, as I described earlier, is a configuration of twelve quartz crystals that is used to magnify psychic energy. The electromagnetic qualities of quartz crystal amplify your psychic experience. The shape of Crystal Heaven is usually oval or circular. The crystals are laid out on the floor or on a bed, leaving a space large enough for you to sit or lie down in the center comfortably. Allow the energy field in Crystal Heaven to collect and build up for at least a half hour before you enter. The electromagnetic properties of the crystals will set up an electromagnetic field within the oval.

PRACTICAL APPLICATIONS

Crystal Heaven can be used any time you want to amplify the energy in your various meditations, such as astral projection, past-life recall, channeling, communication with your guides, healing, psychic readings, or creating. Most of my books were written in Crystal Heaven, including this one. Some people like to sleep in Crystal Heaven to amplify their dream experiences.

Crystal Heaven Exercise

Set up Crystal Heaven one-half hour before you use it.

1. Sit in a comfortable straight-backed chair in the middle of Crystal Heaven and be in the center of your head.
2. Breathe in, clean out.
3. Ground yourself, and ground Crystal Heaven and each crystal.
4. Run your essence energy.
5. Open your sixth chakra and look at the energy in Crystal Heaven. What do you see? Open your fifth chakra. What do you hear? Finally, open up your second chakra. What do you feel? Experience Crystal Heaven for twenty minutes.
6. End the exercise.

You may leave Crystal Heaven set up as it is so that it can continue to collect and build up an energy field for your next use. Use Crystal Heaven when you repeat the exercises in this book.

Past-Life Regressions

A spiritual psychic regression is a guided astral projection into the past of this lifetime or of a past life. Often, traumatic energy pictures in the aura or chakras represent or hold feelings that do not belong in the present moment. Because of its electro-magnetic charge, the energy of the past experience will actually keep a portion of the client's aura or chakras in a past moment, not allowing its holder full empowerment in the present moment. Every experience in the present moment will be colored by the charge or emotion. Readings and healings are not appropriate because the client actually needs to go back in time consciously to reexperience, release, and resolve the experience. This is sometimes called "rescuing the inner child." This statement falls short of the truth, because there is a whole inner family that the soul must relate to. Each inner self has a higher and lower consciousness. There are twelve inner family members:

(1) Inner Child   (7) Inner Brother
(2) Inner Adult   (8) Inner Sister
(3) Inner Mother   (9) Inner Mate
(4) Inner Father   (10) Inner Analyst
(5) Inner Grandmother   (11) Inner Judge
(6) Inner Grandfather   (12) Inner Guide

A past-life regression is over when the client is satisfied or feels complete. This happens when the trauma or emotional energy connected with the picture is released. The deenergized memory will be filed in the client's memory banks or in the past-life columns behind the client's head.

As a guide, you will affect your client with any negativity you have in your body. A neutral and compassionate heart will always encourage comfort and safety. The nature of your questions will probe your client's psychic memory. Because you have projected astrally with your client, you will see much of the truth they are looking at. Being there also assists the client's feelings of safety for comfortable exploration. Your questions will catalyze your client's memory. The client's memory will not stop when the regression or progression has stopped. The special key that is so empowering to your client is the intrinsic memory of how to project astrally into the life in question. Your client now possesses the ability to project with full consciousness into the life in question because there is no longer any trauma associated with it. Future visits will be conscious and will clear your client even more. Your client has learned to have more autonomy and is, therefore, more self-empowered.

Regression Exercise

1. Have client lie down in Crystal Heaven.
2. Breathe in, clean out.
3. Ground yourself.
4. Run your essence energy. Set and balance the energy in the room.
5. Ground your client.
6. Assist your client in letting go and relaxing by using guided meditation such as relaxing the body by noticing the breath. Request that your client postulate inhaling his or her own life-force energy and exhaling all tensions. Let go of the mental chatter by exhaling, and bring inner focus by inhaling. Take the client through all body parts, exhaling out all the lies and foreign energies and inhaling all the soul's truths. When all tensions are out and client is relaxed, begin the regression.
7. Bring your client into the center of his or her head and have your client project an astral body with a strong silver cord.
8. Help your client set the intent of the astral trip, by taking all the feelings, curiosities, and goals of the regression and placing them in an astral box in the astral body's arms. The box will act as a magnet to attract the desired moment in time.
9. With the box of intent in the astral body's hands, guide your client's astral body up and out of the crown chakra, up, up, up, and into a time tunnel. The time tunnel is a long tube made up of millions of rings, each representing a year of Earth time. Guide the client

down the time tunnel.

10. When the time in question comes up, there will be a
    door with a box just like the client's on it. As the box in
    your client's astral arms is magnetized to the box on the
    door, both box and door disappear.

11. The lifetime in question is now all around both of you.
    Give your client a few moments to experience it.

12. Your questions at this point are very important. Act as
    a nonintrusive probe. Allow your client to take the lead.
    Your questions are meant to initiate experience while
    honoring your client's autonomy. Your questions will
    also assist your client in emotional release. Your ques-
    tions will help analyze and integrate the experience for
    your client. Possible questions include: Where are you?
    What time period? What location? Who are you? What's
    your name? Your ethnic identity? Your sex? Your age?
    What are you doing? What is happening around you? What
    are you feeling? How do others feel about you? Examine
    personal and external expectations.

13. A good closing question would be: Is there anything
    you would like to bring back with you from this
    time/life?

14. In preparing to return to the present, suggest that your
    client allow the doorway to reappear and ask your client
    to come back into the time tunnel with you. Then,
    astrally project back to the present moment. Take
    several minutes to bring your client back, directing your
    client into the center of his or her own head while you
    return to the center of your own head.

15. End the exercise.

Chapter 7

Some Special Abilities

Clairsentience

Clairsentience is the ability to feel another person's emotions and sensations clearly. The following exercise will help you develop this psychic ability.

Clairsentience Exercise

1. Sit in a comfortable straight-backed chair, feet apart, and be in the center of your head.
2. Breathe in, clean out.
3. Ground yourself.
4. Run your energy with light green earth energy and clear, light blue cosmic energy.
5. Create a strong boundary to maintain your energy's integrity.
6. Set your intent of purpose: to open your second chakra.
7. Pick a person whose emotions you are having trouble understanding. Postulate that this person's feelings will be drawn into your second chakra. Focus all of your consciousness on bringing this person's emotions into your second chakra. As this person's energy enters your second chakra, simply observe the emotions. What do they feel like? What emotions are you feeling? Are the emotions comfortable or uncomfortable? What do the other person's emotions trigger in you? Do you have any emotions that are the same? Do any images come up for you?

8. Stay clear on whose emotions you are feeling. This is the true test of energy integrity. Notice the difference between your energy and the other's energy. Is there a color difference? A texture difference? Or a difference in viscosity?

9. Separate from the other person's emotions by identifying five physical differences between the two of you. Separate your energy from the other person's by letting all excess and foreign emotional energies drain down through your grounding cord, leaving only your soul's essence energy in your body. Only you remain, only your own essence energy.

10. End the exercise.

PRACTICAL APPLICATIONS

When you truly want to understand other people professionally or personally, use your clairsentience to feel them out. This will validate their emotions. This type of validation strengthens trust, which is a necessary quality for open emotional expression.

Professionals who would do well to understand their clients' emotions include healers, psychiatrists, nurses, doctors, ministers, and therapists. When you use your clairsentience in your more intimate relationships, a sense of trust and honor will develop. After all, if someone has really experienced what you are feeling, that person will know you in a deeply emotional way. Clairsentience offers valuable information only when practiced in its open state. Open clairsentients are clear sensers, always aware which emotions are theirs and which are not.

EXAMPLE

Ed was a relatively new psychiatrist. He was very much an intellectual. His knowledge and understanding of psychology was vast, yet empirically his manner with clients was limited and cold. He would take his clients just so far with their problems and then they would leave him to find another therapist. He did not understand why.

As Ed opened up his own emotional center, he realized that he had grown up in a family of intellectuals who negated their emotions and considered them an unimportant part of life. So when emotions came up, Ed habitually kept them in check with a picture that told him they were "just emotions." He was quite good at rationalizing his emotions away. When Ed awakened his own emotions, he discovered he was better able to give credence to the emotions of others. Ed's courage to feel his own emotions was a guiding light to his clients, who learned to trust and be healed by sessions with him.

Déjà Vu

Certain events and experiences feel as if they have already been experienced before. But familiar as these experiences are, their antecedents cannot be recalled. The following exercise is to be done at night while lying in bed, just before you go to sleep.

Déjà Vu Exercise

1. Lie flat on your back, centered in your power chakra.
2. Breathe in, clean out.
3. Ground yourself, but this time ground every cell in your body. Postulate that each cell has its own tiny grounding cord that is being pulled into the Earth's gravitational core.
4. Run your essence energy and maintain its integrity.
5. Set your intent of purpose: to tap into your out-of-body dream state and remember an event that will happen tomorrow.
6. Open your third chakra up and fall asleep while thinking about your intent of purpose. Quite often the sensation of déjà vu is the experience of a predictive dream coming true. You dream a certain experience and do not remember the dream until the experience happens. Begin to allow yourself to remember your dream state by opening your power center. Be conscious of *all* your experiences, both sleeping and waking. Also, validate

yourself when you have a déjà vu experience, saying,
"Yes, I've had this experience before!"
7. Wake up in the morning and end the exercise.

Déjà vu experiences can give you a sense of continuity and
of connection between your dream state and your waking state.
Once you connect your dream state with your waking experience
of déjà vu, you can begin to own that the reality you are a
part of is one continuous whole.

Leslie was new to metaphysics. She was not the typical kind
of student who seeks out such classes. But her best friend was
attending, and she came as a guest. She started to play with her
ability to remember her dreams and discovered experiences of
déjà vu. This inspired her to develop her psychic potential in
other areas.

Telekinesis/Psychokinesis and Levitation

Telekinesis, psychokinesis, and levitation involve moving an
object or your body without physical means. In the following
exercise, let yourself experiment with these abilities.

Psychokinesis and Levitation Exercise

1. Use a small feather or a lighted candle for this exercise.
2. Sit in a comfortable straight-backed chair, centered in
   your third chakra, with the feather or candle on the table
   in front of you.
3. Breathe in, clean out.
4. Ground yourself.
5. Run your energy with clear light blue earth and cosmic energies.
6. Set your intent of purpose: to move the feather or the
   candle flame without physical means.

7. Postulate that you and the feather or candle flame are linked together by the energy between you, like dominoes. As you move the energy through your third chakra, you can then move the energy between you. Concentrate and focus on the feather or candle flame, noticing a cord of energy from your third chakra to the object. The electromagnetism of your energy can be as strong as the force of gravity. Move the feather or candle flame forward, then backward, then from side to side. Now lift it up in the air.
8. End the exercise.

PRACTICAL APPLICATIONS

Telekinesis/psychokinesis is used unconsciously by all of us. When we heal ourselves, we are using this ability. We literally communicate to our cells and direct them without touching them. This ability can also be used to start a car's malfunctioning machinery or to change red stop lights to green. As with all psychic abilities, the greater and higher your intent of purpose for the use of the ability, the greater your power will be. Goodness is Godness.

EXAMPLE

Famous Australian psychic Uri Geller taught many how to bend spoons and fix broken watches. Some people gained the ability just after meeting him. Fifteen years ago, my friend Mary's seven-year-old daughter, Melanie Mentzel, who is now twenty-two years old, went to a Uri Geller Show with Mary. Melanie was chosen from the audience to go up on stage to fix watches and bend spoons with Geller. Melanie not only mended several watches on stage with Geller, but was also able to continue this ability on her own for several months afterward. It was as if Geller's belief in the ability had both taught and inspired her.

Often, outside of Heartsong, there is a familiar scene of five or six psychics surrounding a fellow student's car that will not start. Telekinetically, the psychics get the car started so the student can drive home safely.

Another example of psychokinesis that many of us use daily is that of changing red street lights to green. If you try this, remember to work with the light's system, first changing a green light to yellow, then to red; then change your light from red to green. Imagine it or simply will it! This ability can certainly help when you're in a hurry!

Out-of-Body Experience, or Astral Projection

Projecting the soul or consciousness outside of the body may seem surreal to you at first, but after some practice you will begin to understand that each time you think about going somewhere, a part of your soul's focus or consciousness is already there. We all astrally project more than we realize. Each time you think of going to the store, a part of your consciousness is already there. Practicing leaving your physical body can be fun, and done correctly it is quite safe.

Out-of-Body Exercise

1. Sit in a comfortable straight-backed chair, feet apart, and be in the center of your head.
2. Breathe in, clean out.
3. Ground yourself.
4. Run your energy using light green earth and cosmic energies.
5. Set your intent of purpose: to have an out-of-body experience.
6. Open your third chakra. In the center of your head, create a small astral form similar to your physical body; this astral body is a vehicle for your soul. To remain safely attached to your present-moment physical body, leave through the crown of your head and envision a silver energy cord, similar to your grounding cord, extending from the base of your astral body's spine to the crown of your physical body's head. Practice going up

in the corner, back into the center of your head, then up on the roof, and back into the center of your head. Each time you leave your physical body, allow yourself to experience all the details of where you are astrally. When you are up on the roof, notice how the air feels and enjoy the view. Allow yourself to be there. Always end each excursion by returning to the exact geographical center of your own head. Now visit a favorite spot of yours on the planet. Again, notice the details: the air, the sensations, the images. Then return to the center of your head. This time visit a friend, any friend, and make yourself known to him or her. Touch your friend's shoulder to say hello. Enter your physical body and return through the crown of your head to the exact geographical center of your own head. Be here right now, bringing the present moment into every cell of your physical body. Later, you might call your friend on the phone to find out if your friend felt your presence.

7. End the exercise.

PRACTICAL APPLICATIONS

Out-of-body travel is a great way to visit friends, to resolve problems, to create comfort for yourself in new situations, or to come up with a shopping list. If a friend lives in a different part of the country or world, you can plan astral visits with each other. Simply choose a time of day and both consciously meditate at that same time and astrally visit each other. The first time, you can visit your friend's house; the next time, have your friend astrally visit your house.

If you and another person have a problem to work out together, it could be done on the astral plane. Simply meditate and imagine yourself going to the other person and talking through the problem. The next time you see the person, you will notice the problem is already resolved.

When you are nervous about visiting a new place, a new job,

or a new school, an astral visit beforehand will give you an idea
of the physical surroundings and people. Your physical visit will
be easier because you have already been there psychically.

I usually figure out what to put on my grocery list by astrally
projecting myself to my favorite health food store. I astrally move
up and down the aisles, then come back to my body to write
my shopping list. There have also been times when I left my
shopping list at home and have had to project myself astrally
from the store back to my desk to read the list!

EXAMPLE

When my fourth child, Cassie, was born, I already had a full
life of mothering three other little ones while managing a school.
Each day went by quickly, with very little time to spare. Our
house was big, and the children were often all off in different
rooms. I would be upstairs in the kitchen, and they would be
scattered downstairs in bedrooms or the playroom. I found myself
running down to check on them and their safety regularly, until
one day, when I was in the middle of kneading bread, it dawned
on me that I could go into a light meditative trance and astrally
project myself downstairs to check on the children. I visited each
room and saw that each child was busy playing, quite safely,
and that baby Cassie was with her big sister Heather. When I
went to check in my physical body, I found that the children
were where I had visited them astrally. I practiced and checked
out my astral experiences with the children over and over again,
until I had complete certainty in it. What a great child-care tool!

Time Traveling

Time traveling is very similar to astral projection. The only
difference is that after you leave your body, you project your
consciousness into a past or future time.

Time Traveling Exercise

1. Sit in a comfortable straight-backed chair, feet apart,
   and be in the center of your head.

2. Breathe in, clean out.
3. Ground yourself.
4. Run your essence energy and maintain its integrity.
5. Set your intent of purpose: to visit another time period, perhaps a past life where you manifested your highest level of creativity or a future life that has something to teach you.
6. As you did in the out-of-body experience, create an astral body with a silver cord of connection between the dense energy of your physical body and the finer energy of your tiny astral body. Create the silver cord with a thought of commitment to yourself and to your present-moment reality, an electromagnetic message that connects at the base of the astral body's spine into the channels on your back and then integrates into your grounding cord.
7. When you feel that the silver cord is firmly attached to your physical body, take your intent of purpose and place it in an imaginary box in your astral body's hands. Recenter yourself in your astral form.
8. Leave your body through the crown of your head. Go up! As you raise yourself up, you will find a time tunnel. It will look like a long tube with millions and millions of rings, each ring representing one year. Move in either direction, going left into a past lifetime or right into a future lifetime. The box you are carrying in your astral hands will guide you, because you have programmed it electromagnetically with your intent of purpose. It will magnetize you into the appropriate lifetime. Because you have a focused destination and are attached to the present moment with a silver cord, you will not get lost in time. Your destination will appear as a door, and the box in your astral hands will be magnetized to this door.

9. When you reach the door, allow the package to melt
   into the door, which will then open. You will find yourself in the time you wanted to visit. Ignore any mental
   chatter that tries to snap you back to the present moment
   and stay with your visitation. Observe your creative self
   of another lifetime. The past may hold some trauma.
   The future may appear as surrealistic images; we may
   live very differently in our future. How do you express
   your creativity in the lifetime you are visiting? What in
   this lifetime encourages your creativity? Are the people
   around you supportive? What life attitudes do you have
   that support your creativity?
10. When you feel that you have completed your mission,
    ask to return through the doorway and fly back through
    time into the present moment. Enter your body through
    the crown of your head and return to the exact center
    of your head, grounded in the present moment.
11. End the exercise.

PRACTICAL APPLICATIONS

When you visit one of your past or future lives, you come
back to the present moment slightly altered by the experience.
Your energy body electromagnetically attracts other bits and
pieces of yourself to yourself. The attraction and subsequent
filling up of yourself expands your consciousness and your awareness of your higher self. At psychic school, some students have
altered their personalities seemingly overnight when they consciously incorporated one of their past or future selves into their
present self.

Hypnotic regression and past-life regression to solve current
problems are two very healing uses for time travel. If you are
afraid of insects, smoke cigarettes, or weigh too much, you may
find the resolutions to these problems in the past of this lifetime
or a previous lifetime. If you want healing around such issues,
please seek the guidance of a professional.

Science fiction authors and movie scriptwriters often project into the future to gain material for their work. The ability to project into the future would also benefit scientists working to discover cures and vaccines for life-threatening diseases; they could simply project into the future where the cure already exists.

Traveling into the future can also help you avoid accidents. Upon returning to your body after witnessing an accident in the future, you can change the circumstances that led up to it.

EXAMPLE

On weekends, our house swarms with children. Usually, each of our children has a friend staying overnight. On a recent Saturday, we had seven children under twelve at dinner. Since I had begun using astral projection to check on my children when they were in different rooms in the house, I had been wondering if time travel could also be used to make the act of mothering less time-consuming. I wanted to be able to spend my time on what I liked most about mothering—enjoying my children.

That particular evening, I had just finished serving the salad and was pouring milk into the children's seven glasses. One glass was near the edge of the table, and I contemplated moving it. "Why not time travel ten minutes into the future?" I asked myself. So I did. Lo and behold, the glass had been knocked off of the table and had made a big mess on the floor. With great speed, I flew back to the present moment and moved the glass. It sure was nice to avoid cleaning up that mess!

Compassion

Compassion enables you to experience a deep, caring connection with others while honoring mutual autonomy.

Compassion Exercise

1. Sit in a comfortable straight-backed chair, feet apart, and center yourself in your heart.
2. Breathe in, clean out.

3. Ground yourself.
4. Run your essence energy and maintain its integrity.
5. Set your intent of purpose: to reach out compassionately and touch another person's reality without taking it on.
6. Open your heart chakra and pick a person whose problems and pains you do not understand but whose well-being and growth you wish to encourage. The best way to promote proevolutionary well-being and autonomy among us is with a clean, clear heart connection. In compassion, we are linked at the heart chakra. To practice compassion, make a simple cord from your heart chakra to the heart chakra of the person you have chosen. With this level of affinity and oneness, you can sense and understand the gestalt of that person's experience. This gives you an opportunity to understand how that person goes about the daily business of living. Remain neutral by not taking in the other person's energy while connecting. This is understanding with passion. You know where the person is coming from and where he or she is going. You also understand your insignificance in that person's life. You realize that individuals can change and develop only by their own desire. Compassion empowers both of you with your own autonomy. When you feel complete, disconnect the cord.
7. End the exercise.

PRACTICAL APPLICATIONS

Transpersonal (soul-to-soul) communication occurs when compassion is present. Practicing compassion is truly the only way to understand the wholeness, the total gestalt, of another person's life. This type of understanding allows you to reach out and touch another's soul. Your charisma and magic are determined by just how much compassion you have for yourself and others, because a compassionate connection between your physical body and your soul puts you in touch with yourself.

A compassionate connection with others puts you in touch with them. Your ability to go deeply into another's heart while coming from the essence energy in your heart breeds love, trust, and confidence.

Compassion cannot be faked. When a heart cord is sent without clean and true compassion, there is no charisma or magic because the message "I don't really care about you" or "I want to control you with love" is being sent. A clean heart connection without authentic feeling is impossible. Cords don't lie! The fake cord connection will drop into the third chakra, which is its truth. As with all psychic abilities, the higher your intent of purpose, the more power you attain; the lower your intent of purpose, the less power and the more karmic bonding you will attain. To use compassion, you must have a high intent of purpose.

True and pure compassion is helpful in every phase of a spiritual seeker's life. The purer the heart, the purer the aura that the seeker lives in. A pure and simple aura is very easy to live in. All communications and actions become uncomplicated and truthful and have a calming effect on their owners as well as on others who enter their sphere.

EXAMPLE

Some obvious historical examples of compassion expressed to its highest levels are Jesus, Buddha, and Gandhi. But don't be fooled. True compassion is also attainable by ordinary human beings.

When I became a mother, my babies needed my sympathy. They could not feed or change themselves. I held them when they cried, and sometimes I stayed up most of the night carrying them around the house in my arms to comfort them. This was totally appropriate.

As my children got a little older, I felt a strong empathy for each of them. Up to the age of three, they really needed me to give them advice. I expected them to follow it: Don't eat worms, don't hit, change your muddy clothes, brush your teeth, eat your dinner.

My children grew in autonomy and personal responsibility, and my love grew with them. I felt compassion. I knew they were captains of their own auras. They had their own reasons for being the way they were. They had their own problems and were fully capable of figuring out their own solutions.

I could reach out and truly touch their hearts and allow them to do the same with me. The intimacy we felt with each other was unbelievably close, yet we each were fully responsible for our own energy. We love and understand each other deeply and believe that we are all capable of working through our own problems. We give each other neutral support and love, which is the act of compassion.

Affinity

While the following exercise is quite similar to the previous exercise on compassion, it is different in the way your energy will be run and how deeply you will touch another's whole life. In compassion, you share oneness, yet you also share passion, a feeling, or an experience. In a sense, you share in support of the person and the understanding of a problem, yet the resolution of the problem or energy really belongs to only one of you. In affinity, both are at one with each other. Only the oneness is shared. Affinity is created with a simple cord of energy drawn between your heart centers. You do *not* take the other's energy into your body; you simply share energy in the cord. Affinity is a state of being at peace with yourself, with others, and with the Whole God Spirit.

Affinity Exercise

1. Sit in a comfortable straight-backed chair, feet apart, and center yourself in your heart chakra.
2. Breathe in, clean out.
3. Ground yourself.
4. Run your essence energy and maintain its integrity.

5. Set your intent of purpose: to be at one with another.
6. Open your heart chakra. Choose someone in your life who agrees with you strongly about something: a friend who likes the same sport, a co-worker with the same political beliefs, or another parent who enjoys parenting as much as you do. Postulate that the person is standing in front of you. Place a cord from your heart chakra to that person's heart chakra while remembering the strong agreement you share. Think of loving the sport, political belief, or child. Together, feel the oneness as the heart cord connects you.
7. End the exercise.

PRACTICAL APPLICATIONS

When you are in affinity with another, there is a sense of peace between you. There is no question about your agreement; you are at one. Affinity can be used within any group that desires strength in unity; it can be used by families, couples, political parties, religious or educational organizations, companies, corporations, dance troupes, olympic teams, and rock-and-roll bands, just to name a few. Sharing an affinity strengthens the fiber or connections of a group.

EXAMPLE

Our nonprofit group at Heartsong wanted to open and run a bookstore. Everyone shared a belief in its importance in our community. Our hearts were linked, and we were all in agreement. The bookstore is now in its fourth year of existence and is run by volunteers. It continues to operate because all involved share an affinity and stay connected out of that affinity.

The most significant application of affinity that could ever happen in our time would be to link everyone's hearts in an agreement about the importance and necessity of world peace. With this collective oneness of agreement, we could transform the shape of our society.

Clairolfactory Abilities

People with clairolfactory abilities have an extraordinary sense of smell, as if they could smell trouble or smell death.

Clairolfactory Abilities Exercise

1. Sit in a comfortable straight-backed chair, feet apart, and center yourself in your throat chakra.
2. Breathe in, clean out.
3. Ground yourself.
4. Run your essence energy using light green earth and light blue cosmic energies.
5. Set your intent of purpose: to experience your clairolfactory abilities.
6. Open your fifth chakra. Pull your center of consciousness into your nose and sinuses. To sensitize your nose and sinuses to the energy around you, breathe in and out of your nostrils for ten minutes. Ask yourself what energies are present—emotional, spiritual, psychological, physical, and psychic. You can indeed begin to smell the difference. What kinds of scents do you smell? Sour? Sweet? Pleasant? Unpleasant? What do the scents remind you of? Separate yourself from what you smell by sniffing the skin on your own forearm. Remind yourself of your own smell by breathing your own essence energy into your nostrils for two minutes.
7. End the exercise.

PRACTICAL APPLICATIONS

If you have clairolfactory abilities, you can use them to "smell out trouble," sickness, or upcoming death. This ability can keep you out of trouble or away from illnesses that you do not wish to have. Clairolfactors enjoy the smells of nature and everyday life. If you think you are allergic to a certain smell, a small test in trance will show you exactly how allergic you are. Have someone else hold the allergen (ragweed, cat hair, chlorine bleach, or whatever) about five feet away and walk forward slowly until it is finally under your nose. Observe your body's reactions as it comes closer.

EXAMPLE

When I was ten years old, my Aunt Madie was dying. She was eighty-three. I still remember the smell that almost gagged me whenever I kissed her pale cheek in greeting. It was very hard to visit her, because I always felt as if I could not breathe in her room. The smell came off of her body; it was as if I were smelling the beginning of her body's decay. Her eyes and face always lighted up when my brothers and I walked in, so my heart knew I had to maintain these weekly visits even though my nose could barely stand it. The smell grew worse with each Sunday visit until she died.

In spiritual readings years later, I learned that a sweet smell can emanate from people who are dying if their diet has been simple and their health good most of their life and if they have meditated and cleansed their energy body of stuck and traumatic pictures. My Aunt Madie lived alone, bound to a wheelchair in a second-floor apartment. She hadn't gone outside for years. She obviously had numerous stuck pictures from her fear and noncommitment to the outside world.

Tone Healing

Your tone of voice can affect others by disturbing, catalyzing, soothing, or inspiring them, and quite often by healing them.

Tone Healing Exercise

1. Sit in a comfortable straight-backed chair, feet apart, and center yourself in your throat chakra.
2. Breathe in, clean out.
3. Ground yourself.
4. Run your essence energy using light green earth and light yellow cosmic energies.

5. Set your intent of purpose: to experience healing tones.
6. Open your fifth chakra and make pleasant humming
   sounds with your voice. Then say the words "I love you"
   with as much emotion as you can project in your tone of
   voice. Repeat these words at least ten to twenty times.
   Next, take the tones and sounds of your voice as you
   said "I love you" and use just these tones and sounds out
   loud, without words. Keep toning, adding more and more
   pleasant, loving sounds to your tones. Let your tone of
   voice play; chant like a guru, saying "I love you"; sing like
   a bird, saying "I love you"; or purr like a cat, saying "I
   love you." Keep trying out different tones and sounds,
   always observing their effects on your physical body and mind.
7. End the exercise.

PRACTICAL APPLICATIONS

If you are a parent, a psychiatrist, a doctor, a nurse, or any
other kind of nurturer or healer, you will find that using tone
healing in all your conversations with your family or clients will
help them feel better. Singers, actors, and speakers take command of their audiences by using tone healing while perform-
ing. Their tones and sounds often grab your attention because
of the profoundness of their tone of voice rather than their actual words. You may find yourself mesmerized by the sounds.

Sounds and tones often express what words can't. A tone that
is loving is loving in all languages. The tone itself is also loving in all periods of history. Loving sounds and tones have not
changed since the first human mother suckled the first baby.
Her coos and hums were loving tones that have been repeated
over and over again throughout the centuries.

When psychiatrists, doctors, or nurses use tones of care and
concern in their voices, their patients feel more comfortable;
this assists the healing process. It is much easier to heal in an

environment that is conducive to healing. Often raspy, angry, or gruff tones of voice irritate and agitate others to the point where they get stress headaches or upset stomachs. It behooves a healer to be a healer on all the levels of word, deed, and sound.

EXAMPLE

At Heartsong, we do psychic healings with vocal tones and sounds called tone healings. Healers take all the psychic feelings, psychic thoughts, and psychic images that are attributed to well-being and whole health and channel this energy through their voices to catalyze healing in their clients. Sometimes healers speak in a regular conversational style. They may sing out different tones, sounds, or even songs or chants that encourage their clients to feel and sense well-being. Of course, all healing is self-healing. Only clients can actually heal themselves. But healers are spiritual cheerleaders, encouraging whole health and the desire for personal well-being through the vocal tones and sounds they use, which adjusts their clients' energy bodies the way a chiropractor's techniques adjust clients' bones. While the healings are taking place, clients have a free meditative space that encourages their self-healing. Clients are offered an opportunity to go within and begin their self-healing process. Just as chiropractic treatments show clients how correct spinal alignment feels, so psychic healings show the clients how correct energy alignment feels.

When I wrote *Opening Up to Your Psychic Self*, I used a tape of Tibetan bells and bowls to regain and keep my focus on writing rather than on mothering my four children or running my school. When I heard the tape, my focus would be on the manuscript, as if nothing else existed. The tones and sounds immediately took me into a light meditative trance. No matter what had gone on moments before in another room, with the tape's help I could return to the mode of focused writing.

Your Inner Voice

Your inner voice enables you to receive guidance and assistance from your higher self (oversoul).

Inner Voice Exercise

1. Sit in a comfortable straight-backed chair, feet apart, and center yourself in your throat chakra.
2. Breathe in, clean out.
3. Ground yourself.
4. Run your essence energy and maintain its integrity.
5. Set your intent of purpose: to speak with your inner voice.
6. Open your throat chakra as you would open the iris of a camera. Postulate that the culmination of all the goodness within you, representing the highest part of yourself, has one true voice. Many call this the higher self, the immortal and divine goodness or Godness of you. When you feel calm and quiet, greet this higher part of your nature. You will recognize this voice from all other voices because it is the only one that comes to you in your essence energy. When you greet your inner voice, listen for a reply. If you feel silly or are plagued by mental chatter that interrupts your experience, simply take control by gently easing out these unnecessary thoughts, draining them down your grounding cord, and returning to your inner communication. Ask your inner voice, "What is my next step of spiritual unfoldment?" Listen for the reply.
7. End the exercise.

PRACTICAL APPLICATIONS

Once you are in touch with the part of yourself that already loves you and wants the best for you, you can gain helpful and correct advice and direction from it for any occasion. If you want to know what foods are good for your body, how to communicate with a friend, what job to take, which house to buy, or which person to date, simply ask your inner voice and listen to the answer.

EXAMPLE

My inner voice first came to me as a teacher, giving me information about my daily place in reality. I had just finished breast-feeding and was rocking Heather. Nothing else existed except the euphoria of motherhood, or so I thought. Then a voice from inside of me began to speak. I listened to it.

"The planet Earth is a training ground for your soul," the voice told me. "This universe is considered a university, and Earth is a classroom where your soul studies the metaphysics of manifesting its pure essence in the physical world. All souls experience a spiral cycle of life/dying/death/rebirth, with each lifetime being a semester, Life 101, Life 102, and so on, until pure soul manifestation in the densest and most difficult energy arena, physical matter, is mastered.

"You create your experiences and opportunities, such as choosing your own parents and life situations so you can grow and expand into the multidimensional awareness of your higher self. You may know this higher self as oversoul. If a chosen lesson or spiritual attribute is not learned during a lifetime, or if death occurs by suicide, you are bound to repeat and recreate similar lives until that particular lesson or attribute is learned. This repetitive study plan is called your karma; that which you don't complete, you repeat. The act of working off your karma is called your dharma, or correct law.

"You create your own reality with the alchemical synthesis of your beliefs, thoughts, and feelings about yourself and the world around you. Every soul comes into its physical body equally equipped with the same possibilities into the same predicament, manifesting the soul's highest truth, the higher self or oversoul, within the confines of physical matter. No soul is 'better than' another soul; however, one soul may be more 'self-realized' than another soul.

"Carried with you everywhere you go, your thoughts and beliefs are a reflection of your soul's own language. Your words and communications are made up of energy that sends off electromagnetic currents attracting like and complementary energies to you. These like and complementary energies are in the form of people and life situations that support and reflect your thoughts and beliefs. In this way, your reality is created!"

At first I did not know what to make of the voice. The information, at the time, was mind-boggling and completely new to me. After several years of cleaning out my fifth chakra, I began to understand how to call this voice to me and how to identify it from the active mental chatter going on inside of my head. My inner voice became a strong guide in my work and personal life. It went from giving formal lectures to exchanging quick and easy conversations. I can call on my inner voice anywhere for it is always there for me.

Clairaudience

Through clairaudience, you can hear voices and music or communicate with a guardian angel, spirit guide, or invisible friend.

Clairaudience Exercise

1. Sit in a comfortable straight-backed chair, feet apart, and center yourself in your throat chakra.
2. Breathe in, clean out.
3. Ground yourself.
4. Run your essence energy using light blue earth and cosmic energies.
5. Set your intent of purpose: to clairaudiently hear discarnate beings (souls without bodies, spirit guides, and astral music).
6. Open up your throat chakra to receive the sounds of energy around you. At first, you may hear the sounds of your physical environment. Ignore these outer sounds and listen deeper within yourself. Do you hear conversa-

tions that sound as if they might be between two discarnate souls? Listen. Is there a particular discarnate soul who is trying to talk to you? A spirit guide is distinguished from your own inner voice by its energy. Your inner voice is made up of your own essence energy; a spirit guide has a different energy yet is attracted to and in affinity with your essence energy. Ask the spirit guide its name. Ask it in which areas of life it can help guide you. Next, listen for any music. Do you hear a song in your head? Is it modern day rock and roll or a classical symphony? Enjoy the music for several minutes.
7. End the exercise.

PRACTICAL APPLICATIONS

Using clairaudience to listen within and tap into astral music is exactly what musicians do. Just as the physical energies all join together to create the physical universe, so the tonal or musical energies all gather into a sort of parallel "sound universe." Tapping into this collected sound vibration gives you an infinite number of sounds to reproduce.

Spirit guides are quite popular within the psychic community. Many people feel they need all the help they can get while opening up. A spirit guide can answer many of the same questions your inner voice does, but a spirit guide can also work for you. Send your guide out to find your soul mate, a new job, or the house you want to buy. Because you are in charge of your own aura, a spirit guide can also be fired. If you do not feel that a spirit guide is enhancing your life, tell the guide to leave and meditate on receiving a new guide; simply will it.

EXAMPLE

Heartsong's lease was running out. The school had been located for four years in a large dark building, behind a main building in downtown Berkeley. We wanted to move to a light, airy, open building in a safer part of town. As a single mother of four children in the midst of a divorce, who was also taking over the direction of a school, I was quite busy; I had very little time to look for an appropriate space. I hired a real estate spirit guide and sent him looking for me. Within a week, the guide returned to tell me to look within a few blocks from my house in Albany. There it was—a corner building on a main street with four rooms upstairs and a large store downstairs, perfect for our growing school, with enough space for the bookstore we wanted to start.

There are other ways I enjoy using clairaudience. One of my favorite pastimes is to hear music in my head and try to copy it on my guitar keyboard. Some of the sounds are complete songs, words and all; some sounds are almost impossible to repeat. It is an entertaining pastime and especially useful when sitting in waiting rooms or standing in store lines. It's as if I have an inner radio.

Precognitive Dreams

The following exercise is best done at night just before you go to sleep, or at a time of day when you can let yourself "daydream" in a half-asleep state. It will help you have dreams of events or incidents before they happen.

Precognition Exercise

1. Lay in bed and center yourself in the center of your head.
2. Breathe in, clean out.
3. Ground yourself.
4. Run your essence energy with clear turquoise earth and clear medium blue cosmic energies, while maintaining your integrity.
5. Set your intent of purpose: to dream of the future.
6. Open your sixth chakra and look through it. You may have experienced this ability spontaneously in the past, but it is, as are all other psychic abilities, subject to your conscious control. Use a simple mental image of a heart

to metaphorically represent energies in affinity with what
you want to know. Place the heart image visually in
front of you, just outside of your aura. Ask the question,
"What do I need to know about tomorrow?" (Or use any
other future date.) Throw your question into the heart.
When the energy of the question meets the energy of the
heart, pictures will form in front of you. Be open to
the unknown and observe. The more specific your questions are, the more specific your answers will be. You may
fall asleep and dream more about the future, or you
may daydream about it in your half-asleep state.
7. End the exercise.

PRACTICAL APPLICATIONS

Even with a very rudimentary understanding of energy, you
can create extensive changes in your reality through precogni-
tion. It will give you a metaphor or goal for where you are going.
Your free will and choice can alter disagreeable futures by changing the present moment, which creates the future. Again, ask the
heart, "How can I change my present behavior to create a more
positive future?" and take heed of what you see, hear, or feel.

EXAMPLE

Cassie was three months old, Sarah was three years old,
Solomon was five years old, Heather was nine years old, and I
was on the airplane with them, alone. I was used to being alone
with my children in the safety of my house, but traveling three
thousand miles felt uncomfortable. We got on the airplane. It
was a brand new, shiny airplane, yet I felt a gloomy darkness
as I situated my children and their paraphernalia in their seats.

The darkness began to overwhelm me. "Am I being paranoid?"
I asked myself. "Maybe I don't like leaving the house, especially
to go so far with a tiny baby and three small children." I searched
my intellectual mind for rational explanations for my apprehen-
sion and fear. None came. Each rational excuse was answered

inside my mind with a rational answer.

As if swept into a dream, with my three children seated around me and Cassie on my breast, I was pulled into the familiar half-sleeping, half-waking state of consciousness that occurred for me while breast-feeding. I had learned to trust this place within me, so I allowed myself to drift off and daydream. I saw a schematic drawing of the airplane. The right inside jet was surrounded by a blood red aura; the rest of the engines had bright royal blue auras. Suddenly, the red aura turned into fire and exploded. Knocked awake by the vision, I realized we had already finished taxiing and were at the runway. The engines revved up. Very quickly, I sent a telepathic message to the pilot, "If you have any question as to the safety of this airplane, turn the engines off and taxi back to the gate."

Within seconds, the engines silenced and we were taxiing back to the gate. What I might once have considered a coincidence showed me again that I could open up to precognitive psychic abilities. Everyone was moved to a different airplane, and our flight was comfortable and safe.

Prediction

Prediction involves foretelling future events and incidents. The following exercise will help you predict your possible future.

Prediction Exercise

1. Sit in a comfortable straight-backed chair, feet apart, and be in the center of your head.
2. Breathe in, clean out.
3. Ground yourself.
4. Run your essence energy with clear light blue earth and clear light yellow cosmic energies.
5. Set your intent of purpose: to consciously predict your future.
6. Open your spiritual eye. Visualize a golden cord of energy coming from the center of your head up through your energy channels and out the crown of your head. Visual-

ize the golden cord going up into the sky and up into the cosmos. Allow the golden cord to go up into the center of the universe. The center of the universe is often called the group mind, group memory, group consciousness, God's memory banks, or akashic records by metaphysicians. Ground yourself into the group mind. It will appear to some of you as a large golden ball of energy. Others will see it as a library or record room. Some see the group mind as a temple with angel attendants in long robes.

7. Remaining focused in the center of your head, throw your question about the future into the cord and up into the group mind. You might inquire about your soul's future pathway: "How will my soul's true pathway unfold over the next two months?" Watch the question travel up the golden cord. When your question meets the group mind, your future will unfold visually. Observe the answer. You may see colors representing certain spiritual attributes of your soul's pathway. You may see a symbol, such as a heart. This would mean that love, self-love, or loving another would be a part of your soul's pathway in the near future. Some of you may experience a scene involving people, familiar or unfamiliar. You may visualize whole scenes, as if your golden cord had plugged into cable vision and was seeing a complete incident as a movie. Observe the visions you are seeing for ten to twenty minutes. What do they mean to you?

8. Recenter yourself in the center of your head.

9. End the exercise.

PRACTICAL APPLICATIONS

This ability to predict the future is exceptionally helpful to stockbrokers and to other future-oriented investors. It is also helpful to high school advisers who are assisting students in deciding which college they should attend. When predicting other people's future, it is essential to allow their free will and personal choice to change the future, since the future is based on probabilities and possibilities arising from the present moment. If the present moment is altered, these probabilities and possibilities also change.

EXAMPLE

I was nervous about an upcoming lecture. I wasn't nervous about the material, because I could talk about soul mates in my sleep, but I had never lectured at the Whole Life Expo before. At two previous Expos, I had been part of a panel, but I had not lectured. How was it going to go? How many people would show up? I was scheduled to lecture on Easter Sunday at 9:00 A.M., so I questioned whether anybody would be there. Would everyone be busy hunting Easter eggs?

Meditation seemed to be the only answer. I needed to use my predictive abilities to see what was in store for me. After the golden cord carrying my intent of purpose touched the akashic records, the large hall at Moscone Center where the Expo would be appeared on my visual screen. The room was full, and there were people in the doorways and halls listening. The images came to me clearly. The lecture was going well.

As I came out of trance, I felt a sense of certainty come over me. A week later, my prediction came true. Four hundred people attended my lecture, searching for soul mates on Easter Sunday morning, and I had learned a new technique to help me build my certainty.

Clairvoyance

Clairvoyance means having lucid mental perceptions and keen insights about people and life situations and having clear visual sight and the ability to see mental images, pictures, auras, and other psychic phenomena. The following exercise will give you practice in three types of psychic readings involving clairvoyance: aura reading, chakra reading, and specific questions reading. The exercise is to be done with a partner. If you have no partner to practice with and wish to read someone else for your own personal understanding, substitute the word person for partner. Simply visualize the person you want to read. Even if the person is a thousand miles away, you can still read the aura from your own visual experience.

RULES FOR PROTECTING PERSONAL SAFETY AND INTEGRITY

Simply by knowing yourself, you protect your personal safety, integrity, autonomy, and free will while doing a reading. If you know who you are, you will also know who you are not. Jesus stated this very aptly when he said, "The truth shall set you free." After a psychic reading, if you find that you have taken on the other person's energy, there are three actions you can take to save yourself from losing your energy integrity and, therefore, your personality. The first and simplest of all has already been stated: Know yourself. Second, send all foreign energies down your grounding cord. Finally, find five physical or psychological differences between you and your partner.

Clairvoyance Exercise

1. Sit across from your partner in a comfortable straight-backed chair, feet apart, and be in the center of your head.
2. Breathe in, clean out.
3. Ground yourself.
4. Run your essence energy with clear light blue earth and cosmic energies.
5. Set your intent of purpose: to read energy clairvoyantly.
6. Open your sixth chakra as you would open the iris of a camera.
7. *Aura Reading.* With your physical eyes closed and your spiritual eye open, visualize your partner, just exactly as he or she is sitting in the chair. Use no effort. When you have the visual image of your partner perfectly clear, visualize an aura around your partner.

   What shape does the aura form around your partner? Is

it a perfect egg around your partner's body? Is the aura
larger at the top or the bottom? Is it evenly proportioned
front to back? If most of the energy is in front, this
may mean that your partner is ready to jump into your
lap. This indicates that that person's attention is focused
on other people. Maybe your partner is someone who
enjoys interaction with other people. Or, on the negative side, your partner could be a show-off, an attention-
getter, or a busybody. If most of the energy is in the
back, your partner is a very shy and withdrawn person
who cannot respond to or communicate with other
people. Your partner's aura may be larger on top than
it is on the bottom, signifying that your partner is an
intellectual person and most comfortable thinking,
reasoning, and rationalizing.

The aura may come to you in symbolic form, such
as a picture of a prison gate, which would signify your
partner's general life attitude and sense of being locked
within life, not fully expessing the soul's pathway. Your
partner's aura may be symbolized by a cloud, signifying
your partner's head is "in the clouds," or drifting in a
dreamy or restful state, like a Sunday afternoon. Symbols are tools for communicating and reading. Pictures
can be symbolized into a basic auric statement. Clouds
floating in the air mean your partner is floating also.
Each symbol means exactly what it looks like. Describe
the symbol, if you see one. It may mean more to your
partner than it does to you.

Auric color represents your partner's moods and
dispositions. Review the Color Chart in Chapter 3 to
help you decode the colors in your partner's aura.

Does your partner's aura have a boundary? If so,
how far is it from the body? Is it firm, flexible, hard, or
nonexistent? What does the boundary look like to you?
Be creative! Are there any bright lights or sparks of

energy around the outside of your partner's aura? What
are their colors? These bright lights or sparks represent
spirit guides. Their colors show the qualities or attributes they are guiding your partner toward. A light
yellow spark would mean a guide who is there to assist
your partner's wisdom. A light green spark would be a
spirit guide there to assist your partner with peace and
calmness. Use the Color Chart in Chapter 3 to decode
the intents of your partner's spirit guides.

8. *Chakra Reading.* Visualize your partner's seven major
chakras. What colors are they? Look at the first chakra
at the base of your partner's spine. What colors does
your partner carry in the first chakra? Go up the front
of your partner's body, looking carefully at each chakra.
As you look at each chakra and notice colors, use the
Color Chart in Chapter 3 to translate the energy. If
your partner has an orange first chakra, he or she is very
creative in his or her survival. This type of person would
be good at starting a private business or creatively de-
signing his or her living quarters. Use your imagination
to see and translate the energy images. Refer to the
Chakra Chart in Chapter 3 to reach a more exact inter-
pretation of the colors of your partner's chakras. Simply
match up the colors and chakras to decode the energy
into meaningful messages. Once you have gone through
each chakra, including those in the hands and feet, look
at your partner's grounding cord. Is it there? Is it thick
or thin? Are there any breaks between your partner and
the center of the Earth? The size and strength of the
grounding cord shows the amount of commitment your
partner has to his or her reality. The stronger and more
solid the cord, the more grounded and committed to
the present moment your partner is.

9. *Specific Questions Reading.* Your partner already has
within the answers to his or her own questions, whether

these answers are consciously known or not. Create a heart between you and your partner, outside of both of your auras. Allow the heart to represent and contain the answer to your partner's question. Have your partner ask the question and watch the energy of the question flow into the heart. When the question and the heart merge, the answer will form in front of you. Read, decode, and translate the energy of the answer.

10. Separate from your partner by reminding yourself of five physical differences between the two of you. After a reading, it is wise to breathe in and clean out with your own essence energy for five to ten minutes.

11. End the exercise.

PRACTICAL APPLICATIONS

Clairvoyance can be used to understand your own and other people's problems and joys. It can be used to "read" any life situation for your own understanding. Clairvoyance can enhance bodywork sessions. A clairvoyant chiropractor can "see" the pictures in the energy body that correlate with where adjustments are needed in the physical body; this can heal not only the physical pain but the psychic and soul cause as well.

Many inventors are clairvoyants who use their powers to create a psychic laboratory first, as if their heads contained bubbling brews and steaming plastics. Most inventors will tell you that they always have an extremely clear picture of what they are about to invent before they invent it. Fashion designers, film directors, drafters, car designers, architects, artists, and stage designers often use the same kind of creative visual laboratory.

EXAMPLE

Lynda Caesara, my first student at Heartsong, was a budding chiropractor. Her ability to move energy was incredible. After a year of study, she began to teach beginning classes for Heartsong. One day, I pulled Lynda into a private room and asked for some help with my neck. She adjusted my neck and looked at it clairvoyantly. She saw that during my first few years of teaching psychic development, I was not in full control of the energy my students threw at me. The old phrase "teacher is target" is certainly true with opening psychics. I was especially susceptible to cords in my fifth chakra, right in the back of my neck. Every time a student threw a "speak to me" or "tell me what's going on" cord, my neck would go out. The picture she saw that attracted the cords was of a certain history teacher at prep school who got my attention by cording into the back of my neck.

Knowing where the cords were coming from and which picture they were plugging into made it much easier to remove and deal with them. Lynda saw the students clairvoyantly as they corded me. She continued releasing my neck for several months. I also spent a great deal of time looking clairvoyantly at the cords, noting where they entered, and releasing the pictures. Soon, I learned to have mastery over how they entered my body. Now, when communication cords come into my fifth chakra, I am able to receive them in the front of my chakra where they belong. No more sore necks!

Past-Life Recall

This exercise will help you remember and have mental flashes about living in other times.

Past-Life Recall Exercise

1. Sit in a comfortable straight-backed chair, feet apart, and be in the center of your head.
2. Breathe in, clean out.
3. Ground yourself.
4. Run your essence energy with light green earth and light blue cosmic energies.
5. Set your intent of purpose: to recall a past life.
6. Open your spiritual eye. Quite frequently in your life, you probably have momentary images that pass through

your mind so quickly you hardly notice them. These
images are a shuffling of memories, some of them from
past lives, which are held by that part of your consciousness known as the soul. For the sake of this exercise,
choose a particular past life to recall—the last incarnation you had with your mother. Postulate that there is a
screen similar to a movie theater screen in front of you
and outside of your aura. Express the thought, "Show
me a past life with my mother." Allow the electromagnetic energy of the thought to flow into the screen.
Then watch and pay attention. You will receive images,
metaphors, and impressions. The more specific the question you ask, the more specific your answer will be. For
example, you might ask, "What past-life reasons are there
for my resistance to my mother?" Or, "What karma am I
working on with my mother?" Ask anything you wish to
understand about your relationship to your mother.
Always retain the understanding and perspective you
receive from an exercise like this. After you are finished,
remove the screen so that you do not have to spend the
rest of your life looking at it by simply allowing it to
melt away and drain down your grounding cord.
7. End the exercise.

PRACTICAL APPLICATIONS

A history student or teacher will find the ability to recall past
lives a godsend for understanding the past history of our world.
A writer or artist may find it helpful in providing the context
for a book or a painting. Just imagine how clearly you could
describe, understand, or draw Jesus or Leonardo da Vinci if you
could go back to experience the times when they were alive.

Your past lives can also give you an understanding of some
of the dynamics and problems of communication you may have
with others. Allow past-life images to be metaphors for your relationship with others.

EXAMPLE

My friend Julie was ready to have a primary relationship in her life. She had opened psychically and felt reborn. Going out into the dating market seemed easier this time. As an open psychic, she was armed with her psychic awareness to protect her from any harm or from wasting her time dating someone she eventually wouldn't like.

She met a man with a boat and a new inheritance to whom she felt quite attracted. Julie was a photographer and could think of nothing nicer than catching rainbows and sunsets at sea, but something wasn't right. Very subtly, the man was pressuring her to speed up the relationship, using his future inheritance as bait to get intimate. Julie wanted to take it slower. After many phone conversations with him over a two-week period of time, Julie decided to meditate and look at the most recent past life she had shared with him. A pirate ship immediately appeared on the visual screen. In the last life they shared, he had been a pirate. She felt this memory explained exactly what was going on with this man now. With a recent past like this, she decided it wasn't worth trying again. She told him, "No thanks, maybe I'll see you next lifetime in mellower surroundings." Past-life recall and psychic sight saved Julie much trouble.

Cross-Species Communication

The following exercise is to be done with a partner from another species of life, animal or plant. It may feel silly to you to sit in trance opposite a plant, but it is far from silly to have the ability to communicate with other forms of life. We live and coexist on the same planet; we might as well speak to one another, even if some of us are animals and plants.

Cross-Species Communication Exercise

1. Sit in a comfortable straight-backed chair, feet apart, and be in the center of your head.
2. Breathe in, clean out.

3. Ground yourself.
4. Run your essence energy with light emerald green earth and light royal blue cosmic energies.
5. Set your intent of purpose: to communicate with another species of life.
6. Open up your spiritual eye and visualize the auric energy field around your plant or animal partner. Animals and plants speak in pictures. If you are communicating with a plant, you may notice the plant wilting and in need of water, or you might zero in on the act of photosynthesis or another life-giving necessity for your plant. You may also see when the plant first formed its species life on the planet. If you are communicating with a pet or animal, you may visualize the animal eating. Is the animal hungry? You may see a name form in front of you. This is the animal's real name. Your animal may tell you in pictures that it wants to play or be petted. It may also tell you who its previous owners were in its most recent past life. Your plant or animal may be a spirit guide. If so, you will see pictures of it guiding you. You may visualize the plant's soul with a human metaphor, such as a wood nymph, fairy, leprechaun, or earth deva.
7. End the exercise.

PRACTICAL APPLICATIONS

Using cross-species communication, you will always know when your pets or plants are hungry and what they need and want. There is much wisdom to be gained from communicating with other forms of life. To be tuned into all parts of the Whole God Spirit eventually gives you the knowledge that all life forms are one; we are all parts of the whole.

EXAMPLE

After Cassie was born, my days were so full that I had to

choose between taking care of my plants or my children. There were not enough hours in the day to do both well. Needless to say, my plants suffered. One day I was in the kitchen with Cassie, who was one, on my back in a backpack; Sarah, who was four, up on a stool mixing pancake batter; Solomon, who was six, flying his toy fighter under and over Sarah; and Heather, who was eleven, at the griddle on the stove. My mothering mind kept sweeping the room with my eyes, always noticing where each child was and whether anyone needed assistance. There I was in my own four-ring circus, Heaven on Earth.

Suddenly, I felt an urge to fill a glass of water. By this time, I didn't question such urges; I simply followed through with them. Expecting the child who wanted a glass of water to come up and take it, I stood by the sink holding it. Finally, I asked who had just asked for a glass of water psychically, which was not an unusual question in my house. No child replied. But over in the corner, I noticed a shriveling wandering Jew plant. I didn't have to go into trance to see the plant's pictures as it grabbed all of our attention: "Water, water." The plant had sent the picture; indeed it needed a glass of water.

Remote Viewing

Remote viewing enables you to see or visualize scenes and events that are far away. The following exercise will help you develop this skill.

Remote Viewing Exercise

1. Sit in a comfortable straight-backed chair, feet apart, and be in the center of your head.
2. Breathe in, clean out.
3. Ground yourself.
4. Run your essence energy with bright clear yellow earth and bright clear green cosmic energies.
5. Set your intent of purpose: to remote view the rooms in your house.

6. Open your spiritual eye and postulate a visual screen in front of you. Ask to see the kitchen, keeping your consciousness in the center of your head. View the kitchen. Is anyone in there? Notice every detail, such as the countertop and what is on it and the stove and what is on it. When you are done remote viewing the kitchen, allow the images on your visual screen to drain down your grounding cord. Then ask to see your living room. Again, notice the details and whether any person or pet is in there. Go through every room in your house, simply observing each room and the presence of anyone in it. Drain each image when you are done.

7. End the exercise.

PRACTICAL APPLICATIONS

Remote viewing is not to be used for clairvoyeurism but to enhance your life experience. If you play with remote viewing as a manipulative or nosey tool, you will be playing on sticky, gamey psychic territory. Other energies that manipulate thoughts, feelings, and incarnate beings play on that level, and they will enjoy manipulating and fooling you.

If you were a fire chief, you could use remote viewing to psychically scan a burning house or building for the origins of the fire. A gold miner could remote view the Earth's hidden treasures. When your car is stopped in traffic, you can remote view the cause of the traffic jam to see where it ends. If your mailbox is a distance from your house or you want to check in on your children, remote viewing is a simple tool you can use to do so.

Another interesting use for remote viewing is to educate yourself about this world by "looking at" all the peoples and countries of the world. In this way, you will gain a greater understanding of who you are and your relation to the rest of the world. After all, as the Whole God Spirit, everyone and everything is a part of us!

EXAMPLE

For the longest time, I astrally projected myself around the house to see where my children were. As they grew older, it seemed unnecessary for my consciousness to fly all over the house, so I tried remote viewing. At first I tested it by remote viewing a room and the children in it and then going physically to that room to see if I was right. I never really trusted any ability until I had checked it out thoroughly, because I was dealing with my precious children. Yet after many tests, I learned to trust my remote viewing more and more. As my certainty grew, a sense of peace settled into me. Somehow, remote viewing made me feel as if my home were a precision watch, with every room and every person synchronistically moving in a perfect orbit. I saw us all move as a unit, together, our souls in our earth bodies as we busily manifest ourselves.

Transmediumship/Transchanneling

The following exercise in transchanneling will enable you to experience deep personality shifts.

Transchanneling Exercise

1. Sit in a comfortable straight-backed chair, feet apart, and be in the center of the crown of your head.
2. Breathe in, clean out.
3. Ground yourself.
4. Run your essence energy.
5. Open your seventh chakra at the crown of your head. Postulate that above your seventh chakra is a heart and twelve loose feathers. The heart represents this lifetime, and the feathers represent your entire inner family— you during other lives. As a complete unit, this symbol represents the wings of your spirit joining the heart of your body, or your inner family as manifested through

your present-moment body. Be open to this earth grid
and its attendant past or future selves. Trust what you
know to be true. The following list shows the order in
which the feathers representing your inner family will
be attached to the heart.

Left Side Bottom Up	*Right Side Bottom Up*
1. Inner Child	7. Inner Brother
2. Inner Adult	8. Inner Sister
3. Inner Mother	9. Inner Mate
4. Inner Father	10. Inner Analyst
5. Inner Grandmother	11. Inner Judge
6. Inner Grandfather	12. Inner Guide

6. Start with the bottom left-hand side of the heart and
   attach the first feather. This is your inner child. Simply
   get to know your inner child. Let go of any preconceived ideas you might have about your inner child.
   Allow your healthy, happy, and well-adjusted inner child
   to come into the heart above your head. Using no other
   chakras or abilities, know your inner child's name. Age?
   What century did your inner child live in? Does your
   inner child have a message for you? Know the message.
   What are the lower aspects of your inner child? What
   are the higher, spiritual aspects?
7. Going up the left-hand side of the heart, attach the second feather. This is your inner adult. Simply know your
   inner adult. Let go of any preconceived ideas about
   what an adult might be. Allow your healthy, happy, and
   well-adjusted inner adult to come into the heart above
   your head. Know your inner adult's name. Age? What
   century did your inner adult live in? Does your inner
   adult have a message for you? Know the message. What
   are the lower aspects of your inner adult? What are the
   higher aspects?

8. Going up the left-hand side of the heart, attach the third feather. This is your inner mother. Simply know your inner mother. Let go of any preconceived ideas about what a mother might be. Allow your healthy, happy, and well-adjusted inner mother to come into the heart above your head. Know your inner mother's name. Age? What century did she live in? Does your inner mother have a message for you? Know the message. What are the lower aspects of your inner mother? What are the higher aspects?

9. Going up the left-hand side of the heart, attach the fourth feather. This is your inner father. Simply know your inner father. Let go of any preconceived ideas about what a father might be. Allow your healthy, happy, and well-adjusted inner father to come into the heart above your head. Know your inner father's name. Age? What century did he live in? Does your inner father have a message for you? Know the message. What are his lower aspects? What are his higher aspects?

10. Going up the left-hand side of the heart, attach the fifth feather. This is your inner grandmother. Simply know your inner grandmother. Let go of any preconceived ideas about what a grandmother might be. Allow your healthy, happy, and well-adjusted inner grandmother to come into the heart above your head. Know your inner grandmother's name. Age? What century did she live in? Does your inner grandmother have a message for you? Know the message. What are her lower aspects? What are her higher aspects?

11. Going up the left-hand side of your heart, attach the sixth feather. This is your inner grandfather. Simply know your inner grandfather. Let go of any preconceived ideas about what a grandfather might be. Allow your healthy, happy, and well-adjusted inner grandfather to come into the heart above your head. Know

your inner grandfather's name. Age? What century did
he live in? Does your inner grandfather have a message
for you? Know the message. What are his lower
aspects? What are his higher aspects?

12. Starting at the bottom right-hand side of the heart, attach the seventh feather. This is your inner brother.
Simply know your inner brother. Let go of any
preconceived ideas about what a brother might be.
Allow your healthy, happy, and well-adjusted inner
brother to come into the heart above your head. Know
your inner brother's name. Age? What century did he
live in? Does your inner brother have a message for
you? Know the message. What are his lower attributes?
What are his higher attributes?

13. Going up the right-hand side of the heart, attach the
eighth feather. This is your inner sister. Simply know
your inner sister. Let go of any preconceived ideas
about what a sister might be. Allow your healthy,
happy, and well-adjusted inner sister to come into the
heart above your head. Know your inner sister's name.
Age? What century did she live in? Does your inner
sister have a message for you? Know the message. What
are her lower attributes? What are her higher attributes?

14. Going up the right-hand side of the heart, attach the
ninth feather. This is your inner mate. Simply know
your inner mate. Let go of any preconceived ideas
about what a mate might be. Allow your healthy,
happy, and well-adjusted inner mate to come into the
heart above your head. Know your inner mate's name.
Age? What century did your inner mate live in? Does
your inner mate have a message for you? Know the
message. What are your inner mate's lower attributes?
What are the higher attributes?

15. Going up the right-hand side of the heart, attach the
tenth feather. This is your inner analyst. Simply know

your inner analyst. Let go of any preconceived ideas about what an analyst might be. Allow your healthy, happy, and well-adjusted inner analyst to come into the heart above your head. Know your inner analyst's name. Age? What century did your inner analyst live in? Does your inner analyst have a message for you? Know the message. What are your inner analyst's lower attributes? What are the higher attributes?

16. Going up the right-hand side of the heart, attach the eleventh feather. This is your inner judge. Simply know your inner judge. Let go of any preconceived ideas about what a judge might be. Allow your healthy, happy, and well-adjusted inner judge to come into the heart above your head. Know your inner judge's name. Age? What century did your inner judge live in? Does your inner judge have a message for you? Know the message. What are your inner judge's lower attributes? What are the higher attributes?

17. At the top right-hand side of the heart, attach the twelfth feather. This is your inner guide. Simply know your inner guide. Let go of any preconceived ideas about what a guide might be. Allow your healthy, happy, and well-adjusted inner guide to come into the heart above your head. Know your inner guide's name. Age? What century did your inner guide live in? Does your inner guide have a message for you? Know the message. What are your inner guide's lower attributes? What are the higher attributes?

18. When all the feathers are attached to the heart, pull the heart with wings down into the crown of your head and know its composite, your oversoul, the absolute highest essence of yourself.

19. End the exercise.

To get a full psychic experience of your inner family, repeat this exercise using your sixth chakra, your fifth chakra, and your second chakra.

In doing this exercise, you may find a past-life self traumatized in a horrible or frightening death experience, which has resurfaced metaphorically. This would show up if you were to seek your inner child and find only a traumatically bonded moment. Drain the moment down your grounding cord and ask again for your inner child. This is where the concept of rescuing the inner child comes in. You may have to pull your inner child out of a tomb, a cave, or the sea. You may have to rescue your inner child from an abusive situation. Each member of your inner family who needs to be rescued has manifested its lower aspects and needs a chance to express its higher aspects. A jealous inner child is also capable of desiring goodwill and prosperity for others. A martyred inner mother is also capable of compassion. Rather than being dichotomies, the two are polarities. Your oversoul is the alchemical synthesis of the highest, most altruistic parts of your inner family.

PRACTICAL APPLICATIONS

Open up to your higher self! Be open to all parts of you, parts of you that have manifested in other ways and times. With this method of transchanneling, you are expanding your spiritual growth while keeping your personal energy integrity intact. When you incorporate these parts into your present self, you will expand your awareness of your higher self, past, present, and future. Everything you do will be done with greater life force. Music is fuller, smells are richer, and love is deeper.

When my inner adult from Atlantis, Alta, was incorporated into my Petey reality, I finally knew how to be grown up and responsible for myself, for my actions, and for creating my own reality. My inner grandmother, an old Montauk Indian crone, has given me a gentle, soft-spoken wisdom and strength to call upon when needed. All these members of my inner family had to conquer the lower self to attain their higher aspects. Nefphsie's intense fear, when alleviated, became exuberant joy. Alta's aloof Aquarian distance became a warm, compassionate humanitarianism. Laughing Waters, the crone, outgrew an impetuous interest in everyone and everything to become a quiet, self-contained wise old woman.

Beyond Judgment to a New World
by Bonnie Welles

Looking back, I realize that my first conscious memory of having a psychic experience was when I was a small child. At the time, of course, I didn't know what was happening, but I was not afraid.

Each night at bedtime, after the lights were off and I was snuggled into bed, I would lie on my back, ankles crossed, and arms folded over my chest. (Years later, I learned that I had had an incarnation in Egypt and that this position was used for burial.) I'd take a slow, deep breath and turn my head toward the doorway to see if my spirit friend was there looking in on me—my guardian.

I grew up in a small town in Indiana along the Kankakee River. It was an intimate community where everyone knew each other and frequently gossiped at the general store that stood across from the volunteer fire department on the main road through town. The house I grew up in was an old, drafty, two-story house that creaked a lot. In a corner of the family dining room stood an old fuel-oil stove that barely heated the downstairs rooms, let alone the entire house. I can remember warming my clothes on top of that old stove before getting dressed for school on many an icy winter morning. The stove also provided a fortress of solitude to hide behind when I needed, such as the times I got my feelings hurt when I would tell my family about the friendly spirit in my doorway and how I'd hear his footsteps crossing the floor of the bedroom across from mine or hear him rustling papers or moving chairs across the floor in the next room. Of course, my mother always told me it was mice. It was clear to

me that this was not the appropriate time to share my perceptions with the people around me.

After several years of the humiliation of being told that this
was all in my head, and years of the teasing I got from my sisters
because of my sleeping position, my "stories" were collabo-
rated by my brother-in-law, who was awakened from an afternoon nap by strange noises. Upon investigating, he found himself
to be quite alone, or so it seemed. He promptly apologized for
ever doubting my word and announced to the family that he
was now siding with me in this ongoing dispute. Reluctantly,
a couple of my sisters admitted that they had also heard the
sounds. But the whole thing was still dismissed by my father,
a Church of Christ minister, as an old, creaky house combined
with active imaginations. I knew otherwise.

Unbeknownst to anyone, I was reading everything I could get
my hands on concerning spirits and psychic phenomena. I was
ten or twelve by then, and in that quaint, rural community it
was next to impossible to collect good reading material, especially
on the topic of psychic phenomena. In most situations, I simply
trusted my instincts about what was true.

I was raised in an actively religious home, and I was the fifth
and youngest daughter. At my birth my father said, "Boy or girl,
this one's my son." Consequently, I spent a lot of time doing
things with my dad. This, or course, included studying the Bible.
By the age of six, I was convinced I had better hurry up and
get baptized or I would surely go to hell in the event of an un-
fortunate accident that led to my demise. My father explained
that it wasn't so simple. I couldn't just ask to be baptized. I must
study the scriptures and be very clear that I understood the commitment I would be making to God. Baptism was a once-in-a-
lifetime thing. I couldn't become a sinner when I grew up and
expect to be baptized a second time to wash away those sins.
So this was a very important and stressful decision I was faced
with. But I was very aware of the Christ spirit that lived in my
heart; thus, at the tender age of seven, at the close of a Sunday

evening service, after the "invitational hymn," I managed to raise my trembling little body from the hard wooden pew, swallow the lump in my throat, walk down the aisle toward the senior minister, Reverend Worley (grandfather to comedienne Joanne Worley from television's "Laugh In"), and announce before God and everybody that I was a sinner who needed the rebirthing of baptism by immersion, as was the custom in our faith.

The following week, clothed in white linen, the Reveren⌐ Worley and I stood in the baptistry in water that came up to my chest. Slowly, the purple velvet curtain opened, and I found myself in the reverend's hands, being pushed underwater and brought back up again, cleansed and reborn, forever committed to serving the Lord. I'll never forget this traumatic and wondrous experience. Even today, I'm very aware of the Christ spirit within me.

So, in service to the Lord I went. In my early teens, I wrote sermons and was allowed to speak before the congregation. I would also draw religious pictures in chalk and display them at the church. Then, after a very angry split in the church, my father and his followers set up a new church on the other end of town. Here, still in my teens, I began to teach Sunday school to the children, until a new minister at the church told me I couldn't teach the Gospel dressed in the fashionable clothes of the times. He said I was hypocritical.

At that point, I really began to examine the ethics of organized religions. It was upsetting to discover how their dogmas limited one's growth and discouraged questioning. I saw tremendous evidence of hypocrisy and an eagerness to judge anyone whose beliefs were different in any way. I stopped teaching. I stopped attending church services. Instead, I held intimate conversations in prayer with God or in meditation with my spirit friends, asking for direction and clarity.

By the time I was married, at nineteen, I had been exposed to even more metaphysical thought and psychic phenomena. The appropriate spiritual path for me was becoming clear. Little by little, my family became more comfortable discussing psychic openness, and they began to read and learn their own truths in their own ways. Ultimately, one of my sisters happened on a psychic by the name of the Reverend Betty Ballinger and began taking some meditation classes. The following are the events of my first experience with a psychic healing.

I recall an evening when a tooth was causing me tremendous pain. My sister came to me, said she could heal it, and instructed me to sit down. We turned off the lights and lighted a candle. She told me to close my eyes and focus my attention on my hands, then begin sending power to my hands, then move my hands close together but not let them touch. She told me to bounce them closely and feel the pillow of energy that formed between them. She explained that what I was feeling was my aura, or my energy field, and that my aura completely surrounded my body. Any ailments in my body could be cured by healing the appropriate area of my aura. This sounded wondrously logical to me, so we proceeded to heal my tooth. My sister started to meditate and bring her focus on her hands as she passed one over the area of my jaw, drawing out the infection. I remember an awful odor as she did this. Then, she passed her hand over the open flame of the candle and the odor began to dissipate. She repeated this procedure several times, until the pain was gone. By morning, the swelling was gone as well. This convinced me that I wanted to learn more about meditation, auras, and healing, so I announced to my husband that I was going to begin classes with a local psychic teacher. My husband, however, was not interested in learning about his psychic abilities. Psychic phenomena frightened him.

One evening, we were at home visiting with friends, awaiting the arrival of another friend, Pete. As we were talking, I suddenly heard the sound of screeching brakes, a crash, and breaking glass. In my mind, I saw Pete's car rolling over into a ditch and catching on fire. I abruptly announced that Pete had just wrecked his car, that it was in flames, and that Pete had been cut by the broken glass. They all stared at me as if I were insane, watching as I trembled and fought to hold back tears. We waited awhile longer for Pete to arrive; he was already quite late. Another forty-five minutes passed, and I was very upset that they weren't taking me seriously and out looking for Pete. Just then, there was a dull thump on our door, it swung open, and in tumbled Pete! He was bleeding. He had rolled his car and had suffered cuts from the windshield, which he had climbed through to get out after the car caught on fire.

In the years that followed, it became clear to me that my psychic abilities were a very precious and important part of who I was. It was very painful not to be able to share that part of myself with my husband. We grew apart. We had other problems as well, and, despite the fact that we had a beautiful little girl, we did not have a healthy family environment and we divorced. My daughter is now in her teens and is very open to learning about her psychic self. Her father still resists it.

I was forced to be alone. Many people would consider my circumstances hopeless, but I learned many lessons. Most of all, I learned to love myself again, and to realize that I was a good person who was deserving and strong. I discovered that we create our own realities and are not victims and that punishment is a human creation; there is no blame or judgment in the divine mind and, therefore, no need for punishment. I learned that God does not judge us; we judge ourselves and place blame on others when we're too frightened to take responsibility for ourselves. In the divine mind, there is no right or wrong, only knowledge and awareness or ignorance.

This massive raising of consciousness is what will heal our planet. Countries will be able to live in peace, and international love will feed starving civilizations. And this is ultimately our responsibility. As souls, we have agreed to work out our lessons together in the common quest for unity with each other in the Divine Consciousness. By each of us accepting the responsibility of ourselves and reaching out to each other with unconditional love, we grow and become united at the soul level. When people of different civilizations can look into one another's eyes and recognize themselves there, no desire for destruction will remain, only the love of Self and the love of the Whole and recognition that there is no difference between the two. These were hard lessons to learn.

In my more recent psychic work, I have become aware of some spirit guides who have been with me all along and who have never failed me. To you who doubt your ability to take responsibility for yourself, I recommend that you get to know your guides intimately. You'll find the best, most trusted friends you've ever imagined, and you'll never feel alone again. When you are frightened, you will be comforted. When you are confused, you will be guided. Your questions will be answered. Anytime you need assistance, you need only to ask. Your guides will help you with anything, but, most of all, they will not interfere with lessons that are there for you to learn.

I call on my guides many times a day to assist me in all sorts of endeavors. Even as I write this account, I am being assisted by a guide I met recently. When I expressed an interest in writing about my experiences for the purpose of healing myself and anyone who might read my words, I also asked the guides I had already been working with to assist me. Together, we worked on some issues I had that were limiting me and needed healing; when I felt I had made sufficient progress with these issues, I was advised to get a reading. I did so, and I was quickly introduced to a new guide, whose mission is to assist me with my writing projects. She is there to teach me how to write and to help keep my energy level up so I can write for long periods of time without tiring. Her name is Heleniqua, and she has a mythological origin. She is very beautiful and statuesque, and she sits very erect. A large, golden headdress, shaped rather like a rooster's comb, covers her bald head. Her eyes are crystalline and very deep blue. She wears a draping robe and sits with a scroll and quill in hand, ready to scribe. Part of her initial message to me was that my body would go through physical changes, such as being able to write for long periods of time without tiring or needing to increase my food intake or my need for sleep. I can attest that she is quite powerful, as I have been writing for ten and half hours at this point!

Another guide I frequently work with is an older American Indian named Simal. He was introduced to me during a healing, although I was aware of his presence long before. I had never made direct contact with him before this healing, so he channeled through the healer and made himself known to me. He felt very familiar, so I asked a few questions and found out that it was he who had stood in my doorway each night when I was a child. He has been by my side all along. It was very exciting to finally meet him.

Simal assists me in many, many ways, usually in a very practical way, such as by helping me find things or assisting me to gain information when I do a reading or healing. (As a rule, I also call in the Christ spirit for healings.) I have conversations with Simal both in and out of trance. He is very powerful and trustworthy. When I need clarity or direction, he is always ready to assist. For example, I was unhappy at my job. I was overqualified and underpaid, and I felt my talents were not being expressed. I was considering changing jobs, but I really liked the people I worked with and I didn't want to leave. When I got home one evening, I went into trance and called on Simal. I explained my situation and asked that he show me how I could increase my income, utilize my talents, and express my creativity at work and still benefit everyone involved.

When I came out of trance, I was very sleepy, which wasn't usually the case. I lay down for a nap and had a dream in which I saw myself in one of the offices at work. I was managing and organizing the agency business on a computer, as well as handling several other duties. I had no prior computer knowledge, so this seemed a little strange, but it turned out to be a great idea! When I woke up, I telephoned my bosses and arranged a meeting for lunchtime the next day, during which I told them exactly what

I'd dreamed. They loved the idea, but then we were faced with finding a replacement for my existing position.

Again I meditated, asking Simal to bring us the perfect replacement. A few days later, a woman walked in off the street who had just moved back from Los Angeles and had all the right skills and experience for the job. We hired her, and I was able to develop my new responsibilities into a very worthwhile department. And I received the raise I needed to be able to continue working there.

I utilize my abilities in so many ways every day that I couldn't possibly mention them all, but here are a few. An ongoing problem for me is functioning within the limits of linear time. I am frequently late to things. I call on Simal to assist me with this situation. For instance, he keeps me from oversleeping or adjusts circumstances so that my tardiness doesn't cause problems but in some cases actually aids the situation. If I'm running late, he clears the path so I can get where I need to be. In the mornings, I count on Simal to keep traffic on the freeway tolerable. And sometimes I'll send a telepathic message to the driver ahead of me to either speed up or change lanes. Together we try to time the traffic lights appropriately. Of course, I ask these things not just for myself, but for all concerned. And I remember to give thanks afterward.

At work, I spend a lot of time on a computer. I had never worked on a computer before this job, so very often I'll ask Simal to help me figure out a way to solve a problem. Usually when I do, in a few minutes the solution comes to me. Frequently, I'll use grounding and chakra-cleansing techniques to deal with the stress level of my job. The people I work with are also involved with psychic awareness, and often someone will be helping someone else to reground or clean out a particular chakra. We also do minihealings on each other.

When people are waiting in the lobby to meet with me, I often look at their auras or do quick chakra readings on them so that I'll know how to deal with them more constructively. Actually, all of us use these techniques in order to deal with each other more effectively during times of stress, or when we need to talk to others about issues they seem to resist.

Whenever I start to feel sluggish, I usually stop and quickly clean out and run my energy to revitalize me. I sometimes use crystals or affirmations to assist me. I first became aware of affirmations in 1973. I was reading a book on the power of positive thought, and much of it was devoted to affirmations. I became very aware of the importance of how you word your prayers; it is important to remember to ask that what you want be brought to you in such a way that your soul's development is enhanced. It's also important to be clear about where your requests are coming from and that they are not coming out of greed or manipulation.

The best example of a personal experience is my use of an affirmation to attract the perfect person to be with in an intimate love relationship. I had been studying many different books, and in one I found an affirmation that would fulfill my desire to remedy my loneliness. It was mid-July when I began meditating on this affirmation. Several times a day, I would go into meditation and, after sufficiently cleansing my chakras, I would begin to repeat the affirmation aloud as many as ten times. I always followed the affirmation by asking that the union we two would create would be for the best and highest good of all concerned. I then gave thanks to the gods for their assistance in this matter.

When working with affirmations one needs to remember to practice patience and faith. Perhaps there are circumstances that must be altered in order to bring about your request. This may take time. Just continue repeating your affirmation and be patient, in the faith that it is working for you. I did this, and eight weeks later I met a wonderful man named David.

Our relationship is strong and healthy. David accepts and supports the person I am, complete with psychic abilities. In fact, he's pursuing his own development more rigorously as a result of our relationship. We've taught each other many things, and we still manage to keep a childlike playfulness alive. There's a great deal of love, trust, and comradeship between us. I'm very happy! And by having this special person in my life, I've found that I'm more motivated to pursue my dreams—our dreams.

Conclusion

Living the Psychic Way

Living Within the Cosmic Laws

Opening up to your psychic self and walking the spiritual path are one and the same. The keys to the gates of Heaven on Earth are here right now, embodied in eternal cosmic laws. Heaven on Earth exists in your own aura when you use your psychic energy correctly.

The aura of psychically open, self-realized beings carries a high energy vibration that touches all they meet. This is called charisma. Such beings radiate forgiveness, acceptance, compassion, and a refreshingly new perspective. Much of their charisma comes from how they use their psychic abilities. Their wisdom and tenderness make those around them truly comfortable because they take complete responsibility for themselves. They never blame others for their actions, reactions, or reality. They don't try to change other people. They allow others to be themselves.

Living in the light of your own soul's essence depends on understanding and abiding by the cosmic laws that govern energy and describe how best to work with it. Psychic energy has electromagnetic properties and so is subject to laws pertaining to electromagnetism. Buddhists talk of walking the spiritual path. The following cosmic laws will guide you in safety as you walk your spiritual path to your higher self—the highest vibration of your soul's pure essence energy.

THE LAW OF ATTRACTION

Like energy attracts like and complementary energy. Whatever energy vibration you put out in the world will eventually attract similar and complementary energy vibrations back to you. In this way, your whole aura is an electromagnetic mirror. You are cause and effect in action. You put it out, you get it back. This also applies to the psychic cords you use and to the psychic pictures you carry. Jesus was aware of the Law of Attraction when he suggested, "Do unto others as you would have them do unto you." Time and time again, we have seen that goodness and altruism are not only their own rewards but are also a necessary form of self-protection.

Selfish and cruel behavior attracts the same in return, while altruistic behavior attracts energy similar to it. Through the Law of Attraction, you can learn to attract what you want in your life by first living it in your aura. If you want to be loved, you have to know how to love yourself and others. If you want to be treated well, you have to treat yourself and others well. The energy of your pictures directs your actions and will draw to you exactly what matches the energy in your aura.

Example. Susie was an abused child. Her core picture, "I don't love myself, therefore I don't deserve to be loved or treated well," was traumatically bonded in her heart chakra. When she gave or received love, the picture repeatedly attracted a man with a matching and complementary picture. She and each of the men she was involved with were abusive and expected abuse. Over and over again, she experienced the same relationship with different men. They all treated her abusively. When Susie brought her most recent partner, Ted, in for a couple's reading, the reading showed that the cords between them were sending painful memory pictures. Susie and Ted were literally tearing each other's aura and chakras apart in a manipulative psychic energy war, a repetition of the chaotic dysfunctional families they were raised in. In a number of sessions, Susie and Ted processed their core pictures by identifying where they were rooted, then pulling them up to their visual screen to look at them clairvoyantly, and then draining the traumatic energy memories.

They then hooked together healthy, straightforward cords. Susie and Ted's relationship was less and less abusive. Two years later, Susie told me that all her relationships, even those related to family and work, have been easier since she removed the pictures and cords that attracted abuse.

THE LAW OF RESISTANCE

What you resist, you become. You carry a picture of what you resist in your energy body. It attracts what you resist. This picture automatically tries to shield out what you resist. The picture pulls and then pushes what you resist. The pull and push often create a silent battle within yourself. You are witnessing the electromagnetism of the energy. On a feeling level, your entire physical body will tighten up with resistance. Your lips will purse, your body will become tense. In extreme cases of resistance, the energy in your aura will flatten and stiffen, creating an atmosphere of rebellion around you. Everything will irritate you, because it sticks to you and you resist it to push it away.

Example. Janet had been a producer on a major network television station. She came to me just after she had lost a job promotion she wanted. As I did a reading, I noticed that she had a core picture of guilt between herself and her co-workers. Her core picture came out of a triangular energy-cord dynamic set up in her early childhood between her mother, her father, and herself. I knew I was looking at her core picture because of its three-dimensional, lucid quality. The picture came complete with emotions, sensations, words, and images. Janet's mother had had a hard labor during her younger brother's birth and had withdrawn her affections from her husband as a result. Janet's father began to focus his attentions, except sexual, on Janet, complimenting her often in front of her mother. Janet was five and clearly felt the shift in energy. She learned to resist her father's compliments when they came her way. She felt guilty at receiving the attention her father should have been giving to her mother, as he had in the past.

With her guilt picture leading her, Janet would deflect her
father's compliments, even when she deserved them. Sometimes,
she would even deflect his compliments to her mother. Later
in her life, she resisted all compliments. Often when resisting,
she would also deflect the credits and compliments to others,
just as she had done with her mother. She had lost her promotion
at work because she had deflected credit due her to a particular
co-worker. The co-worker had gotten so much credit from Janet's
resistance and deflection that her boss believed that the co-
worker was the true genius and not Janet. Janet's resistance kept
her fighting psychic dragons made out of memories in her aura
and kept her from receiving in the present moment.

With the guilt picture released and processed during a healing session, Janet had only fought half of the battle. Her entire
energy body needed to learn another way of dealing with compliments. She learned to reach affinity by allowing her heart
chakra energy to be in the same space and in perfect harmony
with the compliments she felt were true, and to nonresist manipulative compliments. In nonresistance, the aura looks as if it were
made out of clear glass; everything can pass through it as light
would pass through a bottle. Mahatma Gandhi demonstrated
the incredible powers of nonresistance. He gained freedom for
his country, not by fighting but by refraining from reacting. In
this way, he showed his mastery over himself and taught many
others to do the same.

THE LAW OF RESPONSIBILITY

You must own complete responsibility for your own energy.
Friends, family, and counselors can help you, but only you can
change or use your own energy. The same is true with other
people's energy. You can give them help and assistance, but you
cannot do it for them.

Example. John had been a sickly child who gained much sympathy and pity for his illnesses. He got used to other people wor-
rying about his health problems. His mother felt a deep sym-

pathy for him when he was little and truly believed that she was somehow at fault for his illnesses. She thought that maybe she hadn't eaten well enough when she was pregnant. As the years rolled by, she took total responsibility not only for his health but for many other things about him.

John came to see me after a downswing in his health. His kidneys were failing. His mother had died. His girlfriend had left because she was tired of taking care of him. When he walked into the room for the reading, he psychically handed me the energy of his problem. Most people show me the energy they want me to read by holding the images up for my view in their auras, but John threw his images into my aura, as if I would take care of everything for him. I felt as if I had been splashed with oil. My chakras needed draining. I explained to John that I could only help him remove his old pictures and rebalance his aura if he would pull his energy back inside his own auric boundaries. He needed to respond to his own energy and take more responsibility for maintaining his own health. I gave him back the energy of his problem, draining it all through a heart cord from my heart chakra to his.

To truly help another, a compassionate heart connection is more effective than second-chakra sympathy cords. Compassion projects faith in other people's power to respond to their own energy. Sympathy projects pity and takes power away.

THE LAW OF AUTONOMY

You are the captain of your own aura. No one else lives in your body except you. No one else thinks, sleeps, eats, or feels in your body. It is your temple, your kingdom. No one else has a right to manipulate or govern your energy. You are its one true God/Goddess. The final decision about everything you do is completely up to you.

Example. Irene came to me in a state of mental anguish. She felt pulled in several directions. Outwardly, she seemed happy, but she was clearly nervous and hyperactive. She could hardly sit still for the reading. I told her about my perception of a core picture of her needing to please others. Her father and mother had both been alcoholics, and she had learned very early to do whatever she was supposed to do—chores, homework, and so forth—and never complain. Irene wanted to be invisible because the only attention her parents gave her was in the form of impatience or anger.

Irene later married a successful lawyer. She had two children and a lovely house. What more could she want? As the reading unfolded, it became obvious that Irene was wrestling with everyone else's thoughts and opinions about her life. As a means of self-protection from abuse, she had learned to be governed by her parent's thoughts and feelings at an early age. She would instantly bend to their unspoken desires in an effort to please them and avoid their anger. She appeared cooperative and happy to almost everyone she met, including her husband. She was sure that she was very happy. But inwardly she was deeply thwarted. To please her family and friends, she gave priority to their thoughts and opinions. There was nothing left that was authentically herself. After releasing and processing these pictures and becoming more aware psychically, Irene began to see how important it was for her to really be happy, not just act happy. She also saw how she had unconsciously allowed the opinions and judgments of others to control her life. Her true happiness and peace of mind grew in direct proportion to the control and autonomy she was gaining in her life.

THE LAW OF ABUNDANCE

It is never necessary to experience scarcity, because this universe is totally equipped with a potential abundance of everything, including love. When you fear scarcity, you carry thoughts and feelings about scarcity. These thoughts and feelings attract scarcity to you. When you carry pictures of abundance, you live in abundance. Giving of your abundance creates a space that attracts like energies to it. You get more when you give. This is the Law of Abundance.

Example. When Jim came in for a reading, he was working on being more loving. He was a successful real estate broker, but he found it almost impossible to give love to others. A picture in his third chakra portrayed a traumatic bond. His mother had raised him alone on welfare. He was determined not to be poor. His mother had told him she was poor and others were rich because there was just so much to go around. She had taught him a type of welfare consciousness that often leaves its bearers feeling that not only is giving actually taking but, because of scarcity, receiving is actually stealing. Jim was trying to love himself, but he was afraid to love others for fear he would be left empty, without enough love for himself. He believed that there was just so much love at his disposal, and he didn't want to spend it all up.

We processed this core picture. Then I showed Jim how to open up his heart to give and receive more love. He opened his heart chakra as one opens the iris of a camera. As his third chakra released the picture, Jim gained more control over his energy and his life. At his wedding last year, Jim was surrounded in a light pink energy and came up to give me an open hug saying, "The more love I give, the more I get! It's great!"

THE LAW OF RIGHTEOUSNESS

This law could also be called the law of right-useness. When you use your energy for the good of all, your energy is aligned with vibrations of energy reflective of great spiritual maturity. When your thoughts, feelings, and ethics are strong and pure, your vibration of energy is similar to that of the greatest masters who have ever lived. With your energy running at this high vibration, you not only attract thoughts and feelings that are of the same high order, but you are also open to the highest thoughts and feelings that emanate from the collective mind.

Example. When my school had just started, we needed some basic ethical guidelines. I meditated around these issues until almost every bit of energy in my aura and every cell in my body desired the highest good of all. There was no me left—I was like a crystal radio. I went into a meditative trance and placed a golden cord of communication to the highest, most altruistic parts of our collective mind. Within five minutes, the Heartsong Code of Ethics, now called the Psychic's Oath, came through. I did not write the oath; I channeled it. It came down from the group mind through my crown chakra, down through my arm channels as an experience in automatic writing. Once my energy body reached a certain vibration and every cell in my body agreed to its importance, the information came right through me and onto paper.

Code of Ethics

When you are counseling another person's soul during a reading, healing, or regression, you are serving others as part of a helping profession. To establish and maintain a professional attitude, you must set high standards for yourself. The standards must allow you the freedom to remain yourself, and they must encourage the integrity, autonomy, and freedom of your client. Both you and your client are open and vulnerable to each other's energy for the duration of the session. You are protected by your knowledge of energy and your ability to know yourself. Your client's only protection is the honor and loyalty you have toward a high set of ethical standards. The Heartsong Code of Ethics, called the Psychic's Oath, offers basic standards for insuring pro-evolutionary actions. Sometimes, students will create their own code of ethics in the form of a personal "healing prayer" that is shorter than this oath while retaining its essence of honoring the highest good of all.

The Psychic's Oath

I will take full responsibility for my own energy and run it accordingly.

I will take the time to ground myself.

I will commit myself to my body and to experiencing the present moment.

I will be emotionally neutral and aware of which energy is mine and which is not.

I will not undermine others by taking on their problems. I will create no dependencies. Instead, by example, I will teach the laws of compassion, autonomy, and free will.

I will not use my abilities to control, manipulate, or program others.

I will use my clairvoyance to see the truth for each person, and not use it mischievously.

I will read my client's past and present with reference to the probable and possible futures in a way that allows the greatest opportunity for my client's freedom and autonomy while creating his or her own future realities.

I will look for my client's openings, which offer the gentlest and easiest way for my client to have energy, and I will always seek the positive intent behind all energy actions and reactions.

I will create a strong heart connection with my client, accepting my client as an equal human being, subject to the same honor and respect I give myself.

I will allow my client the privacy sacred to all souls.

I will devote my life to the purity and truth of my own soul's
    essence within my heart, and I will support others in find-
    ing their own purity and truthful essence.

I will devote myself to the individuality of each soul within that
    soul's search for health, well-being, and ultimately the Whole
    God Spirit.

Unlocking Inner Wisdom

As a conscious seeker, you will continually come across the
magical and charismatic people who will be intrinsic to your
psychic opening. You will also begin to receive empowerment
by unlocking your inner wisdom with power books and private
meditations, which may first appear as night dreams or day-
dreams. The power books hold the keys to the universe, to the
cosmic laws, and to experiencing Heaven on Earth. They will
teach you how to live your life, who you are, what and who God
is, how to manifest yourself spiritually, and how to attract and
create a personal heaven with your own soul's energy in your
own aura's reality. The parables and poems in these power
books elicit images and thoughts from your own inner pool of
knowledge. Some examples of power books are the Bible, the
I Ching, the Bhagavad Gita, and *The Tao of Leadership*. The
rune system and tarot cards fulfill the same purpose.

During my personal opening process, power books played an
important role, especially the Bible, the I Ching, and *The Tao
of Leadership*. Even more important was the forced meditative
state that child rearing and breast-feeding created. It was this
that became my dharma.

Often while washing dishes or breast-feeding, I would enter
a meditative trance and hear an inner voice beginning to guide
me. As I scrubbed floors and painted bookshelves, I spent hours
lost within my meditations. My inner guidance offered me advice on child rearing and on my own spiritual pathway. It was
during these meditations that a growing inner family of magical

teachers and guides began to show me exactly who I was and what I needed to do. They gave me the direction, support, information, and guidance that finally led to the creation of Heartsong and this book.

Outcomes of Psychic Emergence

The emergence of psychic awareness that typifies our time is a clear step toward an understanding and mastery of our lives. The inner world of the soul joins the outer world of the body. The unconscious and subconscious minds become connected to the conscious mind. Through developing your psychic self, you build a bridge. By using your Psi-Q abilities daily, you are traveling across that bridge. By letting go of stuck and blocked energy, you set yourself—your higher self—free to develop your own soul's full potential.

The most important safety factor in practicing psychic abilities is the cosmic law: Like energy attracts like energy. We pay a high price for negative behavior toward ourselves and others, because the energy of negative, insulting thoughts, pictures, words, and actions creates an antievolutionary (against evolution), egotistical, and hostile world. We gain great rewards for positive behavior, because the energy of positive, compassionate thoughts, pictures, words, and actions creates a proevolutionary, benevolent, and peaceful world. Your personal limits and potentials eventually reach out to global proportions, because our entire reality is co-created and supported by our collective consciousness.

When you have mastered your own lower self (the qualities that destroy rather than further life), you will be living within an aura much like the Kingdom of Heaven Jesus spoke of. Done diligently, the exercises in this book will help you attain the higher aspects of yourself, which represent your Kingdom of Heaven. The psychic emergence starts with you, now.

Continuing to work consciously with the exercises in this book will help you develop:

Psychic Awareness. You will become more consciously aware of psychic occurrences and learn how to use your psychic abilities in your daily life.

Personal Responsibility. You will develop your ability to respond with conscious intention to the actions, reactions, and attitudes of yourself and others. This will help you fulfill your total human potential.

Right Timing. You will learn to budget your time. You will learn how to make the right move at the right time, to understand coincidences and synchronicity, and to use time to your own advantage.

Autonomy. You will learn to govern yourself and to give your opinions and ideas priority in your life.

Self-Realization. You will gain a greater understanding of who you are, what motivates your actions, and what creates your experiences and attitudes.

Certainty. You will develop a cellular positivity about yourself and your own opinions, viewpoint, and actions.

Personal Magic and Charisma. You will develop a child-like wonder and enthusiasm for the commonplace events of life. In this way, you will attract and inspire others by your wonder-full attitude.

Life Philosophy. You will come to realize that what happens to you is determined by your life philosophy, attitude, and expectations, and not by simple destiny. This realization will assist you in moving from being a victim of reality to being the God/Goddess of your own reality.

Realization of the Whole God Spirit. You will gain a deeper awareness of the interconnectedness and interdependence of all people and all life.

Co-Creation

The worldwide psychic emergence heralds the coming of the New Age, the Age of Aquarius. We have just come out of the Piscean Age, symbolized by the two fish eating each others' tails. For the past two thousand years, we have been at war with each other, divided by egos, politics, religions, money, and the color of our skin. The Age of Aquarius is symbolized by a wise being pouring vital life force over the land. For two thousand years, our species will be mastering our vital life force, which, of course, is energy. All things are made up of energy, so we will become aware of how to master all things.

Knowing that we and everything else are made up of vital life-force energy is the one truth, the one commonality, we need to recognize our sameness. We are one species, one humankind, and we are all equal. We are equals in one larger whole. The larger whole is made up of energy, the composite of all of us together. Our collective energy is the Whole God Spirit. In this way, your personal opening and honoring of your own essence energy is the initiation into this New Age, where our integrity is essential to allow us to share our consciousness as one. When we are psychically open, it becomes obvious that it is not necessary to fight each other. We are *one* humankind, not a human race. There is no need to race against each other, because there are no winners when ego and competition are involved in human relations. Benevolent and responsible co-creation within our species, however, makes us all winners. The mastery of both our inner psychic spaces and our outer physical spaces assists our attainment of the spiritual concepts and attitudes that initiate our opportunity to live together on this planet in harmony—open, aware, and full of life-force energy.

As one co-created energy unit, our main objective is to survive, live long, and prosper. The responsibility of global healing belongs to each one of us. When you begin healing your relationship with yourself and your relationships with others, you are taking an active part in healing the world. To be healed is to be whole. We each must remove self-limiting programming, thereby empowering our souls.

We are all souls, divine and immortal, and we are all quite capable of reaching our full potential. To do so, we must each take full responsibility for our own energy. We must manifest our own soul's essence purely in the densest arena, that of physical matter. Each empowered soul has a tone of energy whose sound we have called a heartsong. Collectively, our pure heartsongs are the choir of world peace. The psychic emergence is the first wave of the Aquarian Age, the New Age, a time when inner peace creates outer peace!

LET'S CO-CREATE PEACE

All of us together are one Whole God Spirit, sharing a group body and a group mind brought to life by a group spirit. Each of us is a cell in this Whole God Spirit. If we could get our whole species to think of world peace and to all tune in at the same time in each region each week, we could change the fiber of our group consciousness with peaceful, gentle, and compassionate thoughts washing over the entire planet in a twenty-four hour period.

Let us herald in the New Age by meditating together every Friday night from 7:00 to 8:00 P.M. to bring peace to our world. The following exercise will give you some guidelines.

Co-Creating World Peace Exercise

1. Sit in a comfortable straight-backed chair, feet apart, and center yourself in your heart.
2. Breathe in, clean out.
3. Ground yourself.
4. Run your essence energy with silver pink earth and gold cosmic energies.
5. Postulate that the Whole, the One and All, is a very large body and that you are one cell in that body. What cell would you be? Where would you be located? What would be your function in maintaining the Whole? Surrender to the unity of the Whole. Be your part of it. Feel it in every cell of your body.
6. Postulate that you are within a circle and invite your

family and friends to enter it. Next, invite all of the people you work with into the circle, and then all of your neighbors. Expand the circle as you allow and invite everyone in your city to be in this circle with you. Then, invite everyone in your state to be within the circle. Invite everyone who lives in your country to be within the circle. Then, include everyone in your hemisphere. Keep expanding the circle to invite everyone on the planet Earth. Allow the circle to include every being on the planet Earth. Experience the oneness of humankind.

7. Allow love to fill up your heart center. Feel the love available to us all. With that love as a guiding force, take a cord of energy from your heart center and make a connection with the ones you love the most. Then throw a cord to the people you see in your everyday life, the people you work with, the people in your neighborhood. Consciously make a connection to everyone in your city and state. Now make a heart connection to everyone in your country and then the countries that surround your country. Make a heart connection to every person in your hemisphere and in all the cities, states, and countries in the other hemisphere. Extend a strong heart cord to every soul on the planet Earth . . . one humankind, one people, one world, one and all. Be at one with the One and All. Sit with these feelings and images until you feel complete. Then come out of your meditative trance.

MAY THE WINGS OF YOUR SPIRIT JOIN THE HEART OF YOUR BODY.

Suggested Reading

Each of the books listed here served in some way to help the opening process of one or more of the contributors to this book. Maybe some of these will turn out to be power books for you, too!

Andrews, Lynn. *Medicine Woman*. San Francisco, CA: Harper & Row, 1983.

_____. *Flight of the Seventh Moon*. San Francisco, CA: Harper & Row, 1985.

_____. *Jaguar Woman*. San Francisco, CA: Harper & Row, 1985.

Child, Diane Marie. *Mother Wit*. Trumansburg, NY: Crossing Point, 1986.

Gawain, Shakti. *Creative Visualization*. Mill Valley, CA: Whatever Publishing, 1978.

_____. *Living in the Light*. Mill Valley, CA: Whatever Publishing, 1986.

Gibran, Kahlil. *The Prophet*. New York: Alfred A. Knopf, 1923.

Jamal, Michele. *Shape Shifters: Shaman Women in Contemporary Society*. New York: Arkana Books, 1987.

MacLaine, Shirley. *Out on a Limb*. New York: Bantam, 1983.

_____. *Dancing in the Light*. New York: Bantam, 1985.

_____. *It's All in the Playing*. New York: Bantam, 1987.

Roberts, Jane. *Seth Speaks: The Eternal Validity of the Soul*. Englewood Cliffs, NJ: Prentice-Hall, 1972.

Stevens, Petey. *Opening Up to Your Psychic Self*. Albany, CA: Nevertheless Press, 1983.

Wing, R. L. *The Tao of Power*. Garden City, NY: Dolphin Books, 1986.

ORDER FORM

BOOK $9.95
☐ OPENING UP TO YOUR PSYCHIC SELF
By Petey Stevens

AUDIO TAPES $100 for all ten or $10 each
☐ OPENING UP SERIES

☐ 1. Meditation   ☐ 6. Cleaning Out
☐ 2. Energy Circuitry   ☐ 7. Self-Protection
☐ 3. Twelve Chakras   ☐ 8. Personal Creation
☐ 4. Aura   ☐ 9. Healing Yourself
☐ 5. Pictures   ☐ 10. Co-Creation

SET OF CRYSTALS $49.95
☐ CRYSTAL HEAVEN

Name_____

Address_____

City/State/Zip_____

Charge it to my: MasterCard ☐ Visa ☐   Check enclosed ☐
Credit Card Number (include all digits)   Exp. Date:

_____   _____

Signature as on card_____
                    (required for credit card purchases)

Enclosed is_____

Mail orders to:
Nevertheless Press
Box 9779
Berkeley, CA 94706

Be on the Heartsong Mailing list:

Name_____   Mail to:
                                  Heartsong
Address_____   1412 Solano Ave.
City_____   Albany, CA
State/Zip_____   94706

Books That Transform Lives

WAY OF THE PEACEFUL WARRIOR
by Dan Millman
Available in book and audio cassette format
*"It may even change the lives of many . . .
who peruse its pages."*—DR. STANLEY KRIPPNER

An Orin/DaBen Book
OPENING TO CHANNEL:
HOW TO CONNECT WITH YOUR GUIDE
by Sanaya Roman and Duane Packer, Ph.D.
*This breakthrough book is the first
step-by-step guide to the art of channeling.*

TALKING WITH NATURE
by Michael J. Roads
*"From Australia comes a major new writer . . .
a magnificent book!"*—RICHARD BACH

An Orin/DaBen Book
CREATING MONEY
by Sanaya Roman and Duane Packer, Ph.D.
*The bestselling authors of OPENING TO CHANNEL
offer the reader the keys to abundance.*

SEEDS OF LIGHT
by Peter Rengel
*". . . contains a widely varied collection of pearls
of poetic wisdom."*—PROMETHEAN NETWORK

SINGING MAN
by Neil Anderson
*"One of the finest allegories of our time . . . a story
of everyman in transition."*—JEAN HOUSTON

BIOCIRCUITS: AMAZING NEW TOOLS
FOR ENERGY HEALTH
by Leslie Patten with Terry Patten
*"A well-written eye-opener on the most exciting field
in science today—the study of the body's electrical and
quasi-electrical energy."*—MICHAEL HUTCHISON

H J Kramer Inc

Books That Transform Lives

ORIN BOOKS
by Sanaya Roman
*The Earth Life Series is a course in learning to
live with joy, sense energy, and grow spiritually.*

LIVING WITH JOY, BOOK I
*"I like this book because it describes the way I feel
about so many things."* —VIRGINIA SATIR

PERSONAL POWER THROUGH AWARENESS:
A GUIDEBOOK FOR SENSITIVE PEOPLE, BOOK II
"Every sentence contains a pearl . . ." —LILIAS FOLAN

SPIRITUAL GROWTH:
BEING YOUR HIGHER SELF, BOOK III
*Orin teaches how to reach upward to align with the
higher energies of the universe, look inward to expand
awareness, and reach outward in world service.*

JOY IN A WOOLLY COAT:
GRIEF SUPPORT FOR PET LOSS
by Julie Adams Church
JOY IN A WOOLLY COAT *is about living with,
loving, and letting go of treasured animal friends.*

EAT FOR HEALTH: A DO-IT-YOURSELF
NUTRITION GUIDE FOR SOLVING
COMMON MEDICAL PROBLEMS
by William Manahan, M.D.
*". . . packed with useful information, clearly presented.
For those who care about their lives and bodies, it will
be a valuable resource."* —BERNIE SIEGEL, M.D.

YOU THE HEALER:
THE WORLD-FAMOUS SILVA METHOD
ON HOW TO HEAL YOURSELF AND OTHERS
by José Silva and Robert B. Stone, Ph.D.
YOU THE HEALER *is the complete course in
the Silva Method healing techniques presented in a
do-it-yourself forty-day format.*

H J Kramer Inc